SOULCON CHALLENGE

PUT DOWN YOUR FORK. PICK UP YOUR CROSS.

WARNING!
FOR MEN ONLY

A 6 WEEK SPECIAL FORCES CHALLENGE *FOR MEN*

CODY BOBAY

FOREWORD BY RICHARD H. THOMPSON DMIN, MDIV, BBA

ISBN: 9780985667832

Graphics: *emmy* BY DESIGN | emmybydesign.com

Printed in the United States of America

To my wife:
Thank you for empowering me on this journey.
Without your love and support SOULCON would
not be a reality, thank you, thank you, thank you!
Most people won't ever see the hundreds of hours
you allowed me to devote to this work, and how you
never complained about taking care of two kids while
I was out finishing this resource. You are more than I
could have asked for in a wife, in a fellow teammate,
and soldier on this earth. I love you like crazy babe.

Thank you!

To my kids, Ty and Parker:
I love you more than you know. I pray you see my
effort to live like Jesus, to be a special forces soldier
in His army, and are inspired by it. I pray you follow
in my footsteps with my wholehearted love for
Jesus and sold-out devotion for His Kingdom, while
learning from every mistake I make along the way.
Know I will be warring for your lives in prayer, and I
long to see the impact you will make for His name
during your mission on this earth.

I love and believe in you both!

TABLE OF CONTENTS

FOREWORD

Cody Bobay is one of the most disciplined, motivated and energetic man I have ever met. What makes those three qualities so compelling, in combination is they are focused like a laser on his love for Jesus Christ. His passion for living life to the fullest for the purpose that Christ has given him is contagious. He believes with every fiber of his being that God has called each of us to use our resources for HIS glory. And that includes one of the most overlooked aspect of life in Christ—the physical self as a spiritual necessity.

Many Christians are guilty of viewing life in a way resembling the ancient heresy of dualism, when it comes to the way they look at the physical. Dualism of heresy taught anything spiritual as good and sacred, while anything physical as evil and bad. This way of thinking manifests itself by deemphasizing the physical disciplines, so important to one's livelihood. After all, our bodies are essential for serving Christ to the fullest. A person who has no physical strength or stamina is limited in the way they can serve.

I believe God will use SOULCON as a way to motivate Christian men to start looking at their physical health in a way to prepare them for the most important battles they will fight in life, the spiritual battles requiring to love God with all their heart, soul and strength. In my experience, there are not enough books on the market seeking to strike the heart of Christian men in a way that speaks their language and motivates them to act on what they know in their hearts to be true. That is what this book accomplishes and it is why I am excited to see how God will use it to accomplish that vision.

Richard H. Thompson
DMIN, MDIV, BBA

ACKNOWLEDGMENTS

PRAISE FOR THE SOULCON CHALLENGE

"I am a career Military man having serviced 24 years in the U.S. Army Special Ops and Cody Bobay has finally explored and created a fluid mixture of regimented values and Christ!! I spent my first 23 years amongst men like me who believe in Speed, Surprise and Violence of Action to accomplish the mission - Cody has 'Mission Accomplished' with SOULCON, an instrument that I can understand!"

— SGM Heath A.

"As a Pastor and former Navy SEAL, I found Cody's SOULCON both challenging and inspiring. Cody understands the deep connection between our souls and our bodies, thus challenging all men to 'fight the good fight" for our Lord Jesus Christ. The SOULCON Challenge is not for the fainthearted; rather, for those pursuing wholehearted devotion to God — heart, soul, mind and body. My father wrote me this letter when I was going through BUDS (Basic Underwater Demolition SEAL Training), 'Dear Son; If others can do it, so can you. Love Dad.' Your Heavenly Father, has written a letter to you promising that you too can do all things through Christ who gives you strength." Time to Train!

— Mark Lesher, Executive Pastor, Christ Journey Church; former Navy SEAL and BUDS Instructor

---

"My initial thoughts before I read this book, "I'm a retired Navy Special Forces guy, how is this book going to challenge me more than I challenge myself?" My thoughts after, "I really haven't challenged myself prior to this, I've done some exercises and patted myself on the back!" Now I've got a whole new experience and a much higher bar to maintain….spiritually, mentally and physically!

One of my favorite parts of SOULCON is Day 40...the Gun Range. That initial quoted phrase of Alexander Graham Bell sets you up for success in everything you do if you follow it's simple, yet significant, words. "Concentrate all your thoughts upon the work at hand. The sun's rays do not burn until brought to a focus". I can be a bit scatterbrained, and forgetful, yet when brought back to focus, concentration on the task at hand....things happen. That compelling Gun Range story of Cody's, couple with the Day 40 Daily Challenge (Which literally kicked my @$$) was awesome!

Thank you Cody for the inspiration, through your SOULCON Challenge, to continue challenging myself beyond the age of 50, and hopefully through the rest of my blessed life!"

— Brian P. Calvin, BMC(SWCC/SW) Retired

"Cody's passion to see people experiencing freedom and walking in good health comes across in SOULCON. His enthusiastic and contagious nature is infused into the pages of this uniquely written book. The SOULCON challenge is filled with physical, mental and spiritual exercises that will condition your whole being. They will stretch you to become stronger physically, mentally and spiritually. As a former career Army officer, I appreciate the military language that is used, as it speaks to the heart of what being a sold-out, well-conditioned special forces soldier for Jesus is all about. Put on your combat gear and get ready for a terrific training program!"

— Dale Fletcher, M.S., Founder and Executive Director, Faith and Health Connection

---

One of the big tragedies of our day is the lack of men after God's heart. I believe for the most part, as the man goes, so do our families.

I've played a year in the NFL and have been through some tough training. If someone were to come to me and say they would like to play in the NFL, I would tell them to be prepared to work. You can't play in the NFL if you don't want to put in the work. The same goes with being a man after God's heart. It will take work. Work that's so worth but still work nonetheless.

Cody's book, SOULCON, will push the men of our day to stop passively going through life but rather embrace the challenge and adventure of becoming a man that desires to please our Heavenly Father. Get this book, read this book, and let the challenge begin!

— Abraham Wright, Ex-NFL Athlete

"As a men's ministry leader and retired Army Officer, I understand how men are wired. There are a lot of good men's discipleship studies available today, but few, understand the warriors heart, God created in the hearts of men. Cody Bobay's SOULCON Challenge gets it! I can't wait to see the SOULCON movement take place in churches across America."

— Keith Burkhart, Family and Men's Ministry Specialist, Baptist General Convention of Oklahoma, Former Army Master Fitness Trainer

---

"The SOULCON Challenge will get up in your grill and test your spiritual mettle. The Church needs men to step up to lead in our families, our communities, in within the faith family. Cody Bobay has issued the warning order: Men, it's time to get after it!"

— Andy Taylor, Senior Pastor, Arrow Heights Baptist Church, retired Army Chaplain - Ranger Qualified, served with 82nd Airborne Division and 12th Special Forces Group

---

"Thanks to my faith in God and a passion for fitness I'm called a cancer survivor. I pray that no man faces that same fire before discovering the importance of staying healthy and fit. It's time to sit up and pay attention. Do honor to yourself and to God by respecting the gift he's given you. Cody Bobay's SOULCON

Challenge is a much-needed call to arms for all Christian men. Our sons and daughters are relying on us to be leaders and disciples in the home. We can't and will not let them down. Cody, thank you for the SOULCON Challenge, a battle plan that will change lives."

— Lawrence Lee Lawhorne, P90X Certified Instructor, GrittyFit.com

---

"Cody Bobay is a warrior discontent with the mere self satisfaction of his own warrior status. Rather, he is a determined evangelist of the Christian Man's Potential, who with his remarkable book "SOULCON Challenge", seeks to evangelize other men to step up and into God's willingness to make us all men after His own heart like the warrior David. Different men require different motivation, but all men deeply long to live lives of significance. Cody Bobay speaks with commanding power to those men who, like most of us, really sometimes require more the bark of a drill sergeant than a mother's sweet-isms in order to step into living life at our greatest level of influence. Oh, if only we as men were to live at the level of impact God is willing for us to. How utterly dangerous we would be for His kingdom. Well done Cody!"

— Wes Lane, President of Salt and Light Leadership Training,
Former Oklahoma County District Attorney

"SOULCON boldly addresses the battle that so many Christian men struggle to win. The battle of gluttony, lust, discipline, laziness... In SOULCON, Cody gives battle tested strategies to help every man overcome and become the God honoring man they are called to be. SOULCON is a game changer and I personally accept Cody's SOULCON challenge."

— Chris Spradlin, Teaching Pastor, New Hope Church

"In a day when men refuse to be men, Cody has written a book that will challenge us to be exactly what God has created us to be...MEN!! Challenging us to be healthy, strong, Godly men with integrity. It is high time for the men of our world to awake out of their sleep and step up to the plate, and Cody has outlined the plan to get us into the battle and be completely successful while we fight! Thank you Cody for being a friend to the men of this world and leading the charge into victory."

— Mark Dunning, Senior Pastor, Christ Chapel Church

"This book is a great spiritual renewal to the soul of what men are called to be biblically, it's spiritual resuscitation."

— Dr. Adam Thomason (EdD)

"I believe that SOULCON Challenge seeks out and ignites a piece of a mans DNA that the comforts of our current world tends to put to sleep. Cody and Commander Bugsly are giving all men an opportunity to truly live in the potential that God himself has created us with. This book has challenged me to the core of my beliefs as a man, a human being and a follower of Christ and I am moving towards my best in all three of these areas because of it."

— Scott Morris, Lead Pastor, Southpointe Church OKC

"SOULCON, just hearing that name ring in my ears peaked my interest and made me want to read the book. As a military veteran and someone who has competitively competed in Ironman races, solo 24hr Mtn. bike races, Masters physique competitions and climbed many of Colorado's fourteen thousand foot peaks in the winters months, I thought what was it about the name that interested me so.

After reading Cody's SOULCON book, it was very apparent why I had been so interested. This book is a perfect blend of two distinct challenges that every modern man deals with daily, even if they are not aware of it; the challenge of leading a faith based life, serving

God in an unashamed manner and the challenge of being a physical man who makes time to exercise and take care of their god given bodies. Cody uses his special background as a military veteran, excellent personal trainer and devoted yet humble follower of Jesus Christ to layout a framework and guidelines for the modern man to become active and enthusiastic followers of Christ, that honors and hones our bodies into what they were meant to be, vessels to hold our spirit and advance the kingdom of God.

I am forever grateful and changed by the opportunity to read this book and live this life. I look forward to whatever else Cody Bobay has in store for us as he continued down this path God has chosen for him, mentoring and changing the lives of men across the globe to serve God and maximize the physical body that the good Lord allows us to inhabit during our time on this Earth."

— Russell H. Gray, Lifelong Athlete and Military Vet.

NOTE TO READER

This is a challenge designed for you to embark on with Christian men from around the world in the SOULCON App, with the hope that you stay connected with the SOULCON community for years to come. This was designed for you to grow with your brothers in Christ, push yourself out of your comfort zone, and learn the strength of walking through life with transparent accountability with the SOULCON brotherhood.

Men, we need each other. We need to stand united as warriors and keep our focus on what's truly important during our mission here on earth. We are broken people who are called to follow a perfect Savior with the most horrific enemy in the history of the world trying to steal, kill and destroy our lives, and our families.

During the next six weeks you will face some incredibly difficult challenges, but it will be worth it. The goal of this book is to learn how to live every day the rest of your life with your SOUL in the CONtrol (SOULCON) of the Holy Spirit and not the desires of your flesh. Your family, church, and community need you to take this challenge and grow closer to Jesus moment by moment through every obstacle life offers. Sitting on the sidelines because of not "feeling" like fighting is not an option, we need men on the field and in the battle. This book will help push all of us past our momentary feelings to live a committed life for the Lord in every area.

So please view this book as the first six weeks of the rest of your special forces lifestyle in God's Army. We need strong men to answer this call to change our lifestyles from:

"God thank you for saving me so I don't go to hell" to,

"God thank you for saving me, now please send me into the hells of this earth."

I want to encourage you download the SOULCON App now and become a member of the SOULCON community. This is a place where we will have community, Bible studies, meal plans, recipes, workouts, and different challenges to make sure SOULCON becomes a lifestyle.

With the purchase of this book you can use this code and get 25% off your first order from the SOULCON store:

SOULCONBOOK

I look forward to getting to know you and hearing about what the Lord does in your life through this challenge. God bless and I challenge you to give it your all. In the end we will never regret living all in for Jesus.

INTRODUCTION

Be watchful, stand firm in the faith, act like men, be strong.
1 Corinthians 16:13 (ESV)

Thank you for buying this book and setting your mind to embark on, what I hope and pray is a life-changing journey. This book is a call out of our current comfort zones as men, and a challenge to live as a sacrifice of service in every area of our life. This book is for the men who desire to be on the frontline for Jesus, who are willing to put in the work to be prepared for battle, who are willing to choose picking up their cross daily over the fork that feeds their flesh.

But put on the Lord Jesus Christ, and make no provision for the flesh, to fulfill its lusts.
Romans 13:14 (NKJV)

As men we need to understand that to be the most effective on this earth for Jesus Christ, to live in holiness by walking in the Spirit is not an option, but a necessity. The pursuit of holiness is impossible if we don't stay submitted to and clothed in the Holy Spirit. We need real transparent men, who understand their need for the cross of Jesus every day and are willing to confess their sins to one another. I don't know about you, but I have a hard time relating to the guy who is never real about any of his issues, who never admits that he struggles, and who is never honest about having lustful thoughts. I need to be around men who are transparent about this life being difficult, men who struggle in their pursuit of God's call to be holy. I promise, there is not one man on this earth who will ever say following Jesus with your whole life is boring. We need a challenge, we need the thrill of the hunt, we need for the "boring" Christian life to be a bad memory.

PARADIGM SHIFT

I pray throughout this challenge our thoughts of Christianity change from, "thank God I am saved so I won't go to hell when I die" to "thank God I am saved so I can go into the hells on this earth to proclaim the victory of the cross of Jesus Christ!" We need to be warriors who stand, warriors who are not afraid of getting out of their comfort zones for the Good News of Jesus Christ, warriors who are willing to lay their lives down for their Savior, their Commander in Chief. Before any warrior is ready to go into the pits of hell to fight they have to go through training, they have to be trained in the art of self-discipline. This six-week journey is going to cover some difficult areas and challenge you in areas you probably haven't been challenged in lately, if ever. Remember the only life lived in Jesus is lived by yielding to the power of His Spirit and dying to our selfish desires. And that death is never easy, but it's always worth it.

If you try to hang on to your life, you will lose it. But if you give up your life for my sake, you will save it.
Matthew 16:25 (NLT)

I beg you, please do not attempt this challenge alone. It is of the highest importance to have other men with you to take on this challenge. I understand that you and your group might be on different levels physically, but that doesn't matter. The physical challenges are a part of this challenge to motivate us where we are, not where someone else is. The whole design of this book with your physical fitness is to learn the beauty of development in pain just like special forces soldiers. To learn that pain is our companion, and discipline is not a curse word. Physical training is never, and will never be more important than our training in godliness. But to live as special forces soldiers for Jesus we cannot neglect our physical fitness, because these bodies are the only thing keeping us on this earth to tell others about the message of the cross of Jesus.

Physical training is good, but training for godliness is much better, promising benefits in this life and in the life to come.
1 Timothy 4:8 (NLT)

So don't feel discouraged with any of the fitness challenges in this book. If it takes you two hours to do your 5k test, or if you only get one push-up and sit-up accomplished, just be thankful you started. We all need a starting point, and we all have different fitness levels. Just start where you are, be accountable with your SOULCON team or SOULCON partner, commit to never stop moving forward and remember nothing compares to training in godliness.

WHY A WARNING LABEL?

When I was a child, I spoke as a child, I understood as a child, I thought as a child; but when I became a man, I put away childish things.

I Corinthians 13:11 (NKJV)

I have a warning label on the front of this book because I honestly don't want women reading this. I did this because I am not, in anyway, writing this to a woman…this book is for men. I count it a joy to work with women and I absolutely love sharing the hope and love of Jesus with them, but as men we're wired differently, and sometimes we need a message crafted to fit our needs. We don't need to be coddled and we don't need someone to just listen to our emotions. We need a friend who will kick us in our groin when we need it, we need a friend who will help us fix a problem so we can move on, we need people who can relate to seeing a hot woman and struggling with controlling our thoughts, we need people who understand wanting to run someone off the road when they cut us off in traffic. If I were reading this with you this is where we would high five and grunt!

Now don't get me wrong, I have an incredible wife who I love more than anyone on this earth, but I am not a woman, and neither are you. God made us all uniquely and beautifully, but males and females are polar opposites. So if you are a woman and you're reading this, this is where you put the book down. As men we value women, but please hand this book to your husband, boyfriend, father or any male in your life and say this, "Do you think you have what it takes to finish this challenge?" I promise this will be the inspiration they need to show you how strong they are…remember we're men, we deal with a very prideful flesh that has a hard time saying no to a challenge…especially from a woman. Use it to your advantage, the male in your life might desperately need the push you give them. They might be eternally grateful for the challenge you place before them.

THE INTERNAL BATTLE

THE MOST IMPORTANT BATTLEFIELD

So I say, let the Holy Spirit guide your lives. Then you won't be doing what your sinful nature craves. The sinful nature wants to do evil, which is just the opposite of what the Spirit wants. And the Spirit gives us desires that are the opposite of what the sinful nature desires. These two forces are constantly fighting each other, so you are not free to carry out your good intentions.

Galatians 5:16-17 (NLT)

I truly believe the battle we face every day, on the inside of us, is the most important battle we will ever face. As a man of God, the person you have to master first is yourself. In God's grace He has saved us from living under the power of sin and death, but in His sovereignty He has decided to allow us to live inside these bodies with a flesh that opposes the Spirit until we go to be with Him. This wasn't a mistake. God clearly knows what He is doing. He has given you more strength, more faith, more love than you could ever imagine when you believed in Him. It just came in the form of a seed. He wants to see if you will decide to water the seed of the Holy Spirit or the desires of your flesh.

Do not be deceived, God is not mocked; for whatever a man sows, that he will also reap. For he who sows to his flesh will of the flesh reap corruption, but he who sows to the Spirit will of the Spirit reap everlasting life.

Galatians 6:7-8 (NKJV)

My question for you is this, which are you feeding more in your life? Are you feeding your flesh more than the Spirit? Be honest with yourself. If you are not real and transparent before the Lord there is not a lot of hope for change.

I want you to stop right here for one minute – think of some areas where you are not serving God with your whole life. When you identify those areas, ask God's forgiveness and repent. Now we know repent means to make a 180 degree turn, so if you repented with your mouth, show God with your actions, with your life. This will be a work in progress, and never accept failure in this area. As soon as men of God accept they cannot overcome an area of weakness, they slowly start to be overcome by that weakness. The purpose God has for this book and challenge in your life is to inspire you to be men of courage, to be men who strive daily to be more like Christ and less like the you before Christ. This process will take a lifetime...this process is called sanctification.

SANCTIFICATION

> Don't you realize that your body is the temple of the Holy Spirit, who lives in you and was given to you by God? You do not belong to yourself, for God bought you with a high price. So you must honor God with your body.
>
> 1 Corinthians 6:19-20 (NLT)

As Christian men we like to compartmentalize life. Somehow we have compartmentalized our physical bodies out of the work of sanctification when it should be one of the main focuses of sanctification. Think about it. If you use your body for a little sexual pleasure, is that okay? Well, if you are married and it is in the confines of marriage absolutely! It is a wonderful thing! But if you are married, and you masturbate while thinking about another woman, we all know that is not in line with God's call to be holy like He is holy. What about eating? Why is it acceptable for Christian men to eat unhealthy and not exercise? To feed the desire of our flesh is laziness and gluttony. God cares about the overall health of your body and how we steward the temple His Spirit lives in, and we should too. We must remember it is by the desires of our own flesh that we are tempted, and it is by denying those desires that we will either grow closer to God or further from Him by feeding those unholy desires.

Now I have to clarify one thing here, nothing you do will ever separate you from the love of God, but our actions can separate us from feeling and experiencing God's love. And that love helps us transform our lives and gives us the power and confidence to share the love with everyone around us. As special forces soldiers in

Jesus's army, the unconditional love of Jesus that He showed us on the cross is our secret weapon! We have to share it with everyone we come in contact with...

> And I am convinced that nothing can ever separate us from God's love. Neither death nor life, neither angels nor demons, neither our fears for today nor our worries about tomorrow— not even the powers of hell can separate us from God's love. No power in the sky above or in the earth below—indeed, nothing in all creation will ever be able to separate us from the love of God that is revealed in Christ Jesus our Lord.
>
> Romans 8:38-39 (NLT)

And as we share this love with people in our lives we can never forget that God loved us just as we were before we knew Him, and He loves everyone with that same passionate love. We have to share this message, even if it means giving up our lives. If we don't, who will? We have to take the light of the Gospel and light up the world around us. And we have to be willing to endure the persecution, shame and suffering that comes along with advancing the Gospel. None of the negative emotions compare with the joy of doing God's work. Nothing compares with the intimacy of walking with Jesus daily...

PUT DOWN YOUR FORK & PICK UP YOUR CROSS

A CALL TO SACRIFICE, NOT COMFORT

If by excessive labor, we die before the average age of man, worn out in the Master's service, then glory be to God, we shall have so much less of earth and so much more of Heaven... It is our duty and our privilege to exhaust our lives for Jesus. We are not to be living specimens of men in fine preservation, but living sacrifices, whose lot is to be consumed.

Charles Spurgeon

This challenge is specifically for the man who is a warrior on the inside, the man who longs for the fight, the man who desires to please God but constantly struggles. If that's you, you are going to truly enjoy this challenge with brothers just like you.

I join the ranks with everyone reading this about the difficulty of submitting to the Holy Spirit and pursuing Christ with my entire life. There are so many areas where I am selfish, where I would rather coddle my flesh than crucify it. But that's not what Jesus calls us to do. Jesus calls us to come and die, daily, because He knows when we die to ourselves, it's the only way we will ever truly live.

If any of you wants to be my follower, you must turn from your selfish ways, take up your cross daily, and follow Me. For whoever desires to save his life will lose it, but whoever loses his life for My sake will save it.

Luke 9:23-24 (NKJV)

There are a lot of people that say and preach that following Jesus is easy and always enjoyable. Those people must have overlooked this passage. To me, I hear it as one of the most challenging things Jesus ever said. This is a challenge from our Commander in Chief to live like He lived on this earth – to live to please God and not ourselves. To submit the control of our mind, our will, and our emotions to the Holy Spirit daily. A challenge to live to love God and love others by laying our lives down for them just like Jesus did. Now most of us probably won't ever be physically crucified, but we are all responsible for choosing to crucify our flesh daily by yielding control to the Holy Spirit. This means putting to death the desire to feed any area of our flesh instead of the Holy Spirit of God inside of us. The hard fact is we have so many men who could be elite special forces soldiers in the Body of Christ, but are living under the control of their flesh. We have men who could be on the frontlines for Jesus that are on the homepage of the latest porn website. We have men who should be looking for areas to serve others, but they are too busy eating fast food on their recliners, living under the control of their appetites. We need an awakening, we need a revolution in the Body of Christ, and that revolution starts with us. We have to answer the call of self-discipline, we have to let Jesus know we're ready to live all in for Him and what He desires. And that starts by submitting our entire lives to His Spirit, daily. Only then will we truly live.

I served this country for six years on active duty in the military and there is one thing I know for sure: pride, gluttony, and laziness are three things that have no part in the life of an elite soldier. Soldiers who want to be elite go through some of the most difficult training this country has to offer, and for what? They want to be counted worthy to live with the purpose of defending this country, and they are always ready to die for their faith in the country they serve. It's time we stand like this for the Kingdom of God!

I challenge you to look at your life, and find the areas where you have fed your flesh to a stronger degree than the Spirit. Maybe you're using your fork to feed your flesh with a pornography addiction, maybe anger issues, maybe your appetite for food, or maybe there's another desire of your flesh that you have been feeding bite by bite with your fork. Those areas where you have not submitted control to the Holy Spirit, the areas that maybe no one knows but you, those areas need to be starved to death and crucified. This is a battle you cannot win in your own strength. You need the Holy Spirit and the accountability of Godly men in your life.

Throughout this challenge our focus will continually be growing stronger in the Spirit by denying the fork that feeds our flesh and picking up our cross daily. This world needs men willing and ready to say, "here I am Lord, send me into the darkness, I am submitted to the Spirit, highly trained, disciplined, and ready for war." By the end of this challenge I pray the Lord looks at all of us and says:

You're ready. You're trained now more than ever in submitting to the Holy Spirit over the desires of your flesh. Welcome to the Special Forces Team in the Kingdom of Heaven. Let's go proclaim the victory of the cross to everyone on earth … and don't worry, no matter how dark it gets, I will never leave you or forsake you.

WEAPONS OF MASS DESTRUCTION

For God has not given us a spirit of fear and timidity, but of power, love, and self-discipline.

2 Timothy 1:7 (NLT)

Living a life dedicated to the mission the Lord has given us is the only place we will find the strength to live as a sacrifice of service to God. This is not a mission with rainbows and butterflies, this is a mission of force to help people suffering on this earth, to bring hope to the hopeless, to love the unlovely, and oh yeah, there's a highly trained enemy waiting to use your flesh to strategically put you on the sidelines, or ideally in the grave.

There is a daily battle for your soul (mind, will and emotions) and it is imperative we learn how to live in victory with this battle. Jesus came to this earth, lived a perfect life, died a horrible death on a cross, and rose from the grave so He could give us spiritual life. He gave us the best gift we could ask for, the Holy Spirit. In the Holy Spirit we are born again, and it's the only place we have life, and everywhere else is death. In Him we have every weapon needed to live in victory over the schemes of darkness on this earth. But the Holy Spirit gives us the choice to either use His weapons of warfare or our own.

Let's take some time and look at the main weapons used in the battle to sanctify our mind, will, and emotions on this earth.

THE CROSS

If anyone desires to come after Me, let him deny himself, and take up his cross daily, and follow Me.

Luke 9:23 (NKJV)

I want to take just a moment to make sure we are on the same page with this passage before we go forward. At the time when Jesus said this to His disciples the cross was a tool for public shame, suffering, justice for a crime and the end result being a slow painful death. The disciples didn't know that Jesus was going to take that symbol and change the outcome of the cross forever. So it is imperative that we have a clear view of the cross that Jesus is telling us to pick up daily. As believers in Jesus we now know the end result of the cross is victory, and a victory for humanity we could never obtain on our own. The cross reminds us of the horribly painful death Jesus went through for our sins. If any human could have lived a sinless life and poured out their blood on a cross for the forgiveness of our sins, then Jesus wouldn't have had to come to this earth to die for us. God knew for the human race to have forgiveness for their sins and experience true life on this earth and throughout eternity, Jesus's innocent blood had to be shed on the cross for us. And Jesus went through the excruciating pain of the cross for the joy of having an eternal personal relationship with people like you and me.

...Because of the joy awaiting him, he endured the cross, disregarding its shame. Now he is seated in the place of honor beside God's throne.

Hebrews 12:2b (NLT)

Our King died in our place, and He is asking us to make the decision to pick up our cross and follow Him. What an incredible honor. The cross is our symbol of victory, our symbol from our Savior of what true love is, and our symbol that our Commander in Chief laid down His life for us. Just take a moment and think if a world leader made the decision to give their life for yours. Wouldn't you live to bring honor to that person's life? Absolutely! And that is why we count it an honor to pick up our cross and honor God by obeying Him and suffering for Him.

The world cries for men who are strong; strong in conviction, strong to lead, to stand, to suffer.

Elisabeth Elliot

When we make the decision to pick up our cross and follow Jesus we are showing God we are all in. We are showing Him we are willing to bring honor to Him and His Kingdom no matter what the cost. We are showing Him we desire to be special forces soldiers in His army.

In America today the cross has lost much of its true message. We constantly see stars on television wearing crosses that are singing or talking about things that completely contradict the Bible. We see the cross used as décor in homes and on t-shirts. But the cross is not just a decoration, the cross is what defines the Christian. The cross is both a reminder of the depth of our sin, that our sin was so bad Jesus had to die for us; and at the same time it's our symbol of the depth of God's unconditional love for us. The cross is empty, that means Jesus is resurrected, He conquered the grave, and He is waiting for us to repent and accept His sacrifice. Once we do, we are spiritually born again, we gain the understanding that the cross of Jesus saved our lives. Our sin is and was so wretched the Son of God had to die for us. Now, the cross shows us victory over darkness…any and every kind of darkness. When our view of the end result of the cross is constantly a symbol of victory, forgiveness, unconditional love, hope, and strength that we could never have on our own, our lives become drastically different. But even though the end result of the cross has changed, the suffering, shame and death in carrying the cross hasn't changed. The call to pick up our cross daily is one of giving up everything to follow Jesus. Being willing to go through hell on earth for the Gospel with the focus and hope of seeing God save people from hell on earth and throughout eternity. It is crucial we work to live unashamed of Jesus Christ every day, and it is impossible to do that without picking up our cross daily and following Him. It is crucial we start today and make a stand as Christian men, a stand to accept the call to self-sacrifice and kill our desires to simply live a comfortable life. For the Kingdom of God and for the sake of our families men, it is crucial.

For I am not ashamed of the gospel of Christ, for it is the power of God to salvation for everyone who believes.

Romans 1:16a (NKJV)

THE STAND

Therefore, brethren, we are debtors—not to the flesh, to live according to the flesh. For if you live according to the flesh you will die; but if by the Spirit you put to death the deeds of the body, you will live.

Romans 8:12-13 (NKJV)

The first and main step of the stand that needs to be made starts on our knees every morning. This stand is submitting our lives daily to the Holy Spirit and living the life He desires for us and not the lives we desire – the good news is what God desires is far better than anything we could muster up in our own strength and mind. Throughout this challenge we will focus on starting each morning on our knees praying the Lord's Prayer. This is one of the fundamentals in the life of an elite warrior of Jesus that we need to practice daily, and we need to hold each other accountable with our prayer lives as men. I cannot tell you how many married men (including myself) feel awkward when their wives come in the room and they are on their knees praying. Guys, we need to reverse this. Our wives should start to see a boldness in our lives for Jesus that will continue to grow stronger. We need to come to a place where our actions start to reflect the life of Jesus. Our families, our friends, and this world need our leadership in this area.

The second step we will focus on throughout this challenge is sharing the Good News of the power of the cross with as many people as possible. It is important here that we understand that we cannot share what we do not have. That is why it is so important we are spending time on our knees in prayer every morning focusing on the victory of the cross and God's incredible, unconditional love for our lives. When we do this, when we keep our focus locked in on these things, an overwhelming desire will fill our hearts of God's amazing grace…and our only option will be to share that with the people in our lives. This world needs men to courageously take the message of the cross to every dark place in this world. Men willing to pick up their cross every morning, unashamed of the Gospel, and fully aware of the meaning of the cross they carry. This world needs men who are more passionate about sharing the Good News that will save someone from hell than living to stay in their own comfort zones. Men, this world needs us to go all in for Jesus.

For God so loved the world that He gave His only begotten Son, that whoever believes in Him should not perish but have everlasting life. For God did not send His Son into the world to condemn the world, but that the world through Him might be saved.

John 3:16-17 (NKJV)

OUR CHOICE

In any branch of the military there are different jobs with unique missions. There are some people who are assigned to do the ordinary tasks with little danger, but then there are some people who long for a life of danger, and long to be out in the battle. There are some people who desire to be used by the government as a special force. But just because someone wants to be in the battle, used by the government as a special force, doesn't mean they won't have to train. As a matter of fact they have to train harder than anyone else, they suffer more than anyone else, but their eyes are fixed on the end goal, the goal of living a life of courage, honor, and being elite for their country. The Kingdom of Heaven is the same way. Before Jesus trusts us with top secret, highly dangerous missions, He has to see that we are developing in the knowledge of everything the cross of Jesus Christ represents. God has to look at us and see that we take this Christian life seriously, and we live in honor of His name. Committed soldiers of the cross of Jesus should be focused on one thing, their God given mission. Period. And that mission lives and dies on the message of the grace, hope and unconditional love found in the cross of Jesus. I believe God is working right now in your heart and asking you, "Do you want to be used as a special force on this earth?" No matter what your answer is, God will love you the same, but your answer determines how God will use you on this earth. Hear what the Apostle Paul wrote to Timothy in his last book:

You therefore, my son, be strong in the grace that is in Christ Jesus. And the things that you have heard from me among many witnesses, commit these to faithful men who will be able to teach others also. You therefore must endure hardship as a good soldier of Jesus Christ. No one engaged in warfare entangles himself with the affairs of this life, that he may please him who enlisted him as a soldier. And also if anyone competes in athletics, he is not crowned unless he competes according to the rules. The hardworking farmer must be first to partake of the crops. Consider what I say, and may the Lord give you understanding in all things. Remember that Jesus Christ, of the seed of David, was raised from the dead according to my gospel, for which I suffer trouble as an evildoer, even to the point of chains; but the word of God is not chained. Therefore

I endure all things for the sake of the elect, that they also may obtain the salvation which is in Christ Jesus with eternal glory. This is a faithful saying:

For if we died with Him, We shall also live with Him.
If we endure, We shall also reign with Him.
If we deny Him, He also will deny us.
If we are faithless,
He remains faithful;
He cannot deny Himself.

Remind them of these things, charging them before the Lord not to strive about words to no profit, to the ruin of the hearers. Be diligent to present yourself approved to God, a worker who does not need to be ashamed, rightly dividing the word of truth. But shun profane and idle babblings, for they will increase to more ungodliness. And their message will spread like cancer. Hymenaeus and Philetus are of this sort, who have strayed concerning the truth, saying that the resurrection is already past; and they overthrow the faith of some. Nevertheless the solid foundation of God stands, having this seal:

'The Lord knows those who are His,' and, 'Let everyone who names the name of Christ depart from iniquity.'

But in a great house there are not only vessels of gold and silver, but also of wood and clay, some for honor and some for dishonor. Therefore if anyone cleanses himself from the latter, he will be a vessel for honor, sanctified and useful for the Master, prepared for every good work. Flee also youthful lusts; but pursue righteousness, faith, love, peace with those who call on the Lord out of a pure heart. But avoid foolish and ignorant disputes, knowing that they generate strife. And a servant of the Lord must not quarrel but be gentle to all, able to teach, patient, in humility correcting those who are in opposition, if God perhaps will grant them repentance, so that they may know the truth, and that they may come to their senses and escape the snare of the devil, having been taken captive by him to do his will.

2 Timothy 2 (NKJV)

We need more men to be set apart, to be committed soldiers of Jesus Christ. Men who are ready to stand for their Savior to the death, and men who are willing to exhaust their lives for the Good News. There are people who are living in hell on earth that could be eternally impacted by hearing the amazing grace of the cross. I don't know about you, but I don't want to stand before the Lord and know the person living right next to me didn't know about the cross of Jesus and I could have taken time out of my "busy" life and shared that eternity changing message with them.

What would this world look like if every Christian man lived with a sense of urgency and passion to evangelize the Gospel to the people in their lives? Men who would be willing to look like fools for Jesus, men who are excited to tell people about the beauty, power, hope, love and healing of the cross. I believe once we cross over the line of being afraid of looking foolish for Jesus, we will see His power start to fall in our lives like never before. This world needs us to live unashamed of the Gospel.

> *For I am not ashamed of the gospel of Christ, for it is the power of God to salvation for everyone who believes.*
>
> Romans 1:16a (NKJV)

When the cross becomes our main focus, we start to experience the victory of Jesus in every area of life. The cross is the most powerful weapon on the face of this earth for the Kingdom of Heaven. Without the cross we wouldn't have our salvation bought by the precious blood of Jesus and we wouldn't have the best gift in the world, the Holy Spirit. We are redeemed because our Savior died on the cross in our place to pay the ultimate sacrifice for our sins, and He did it because He loves us like crazy and He desires for all men to know Him. It is our responsibility and joy to share the message of His love and His victory over the cross with everyone we come in contact with, either through word or deed. We have to make sure nothing slows us down or stops us, and we have to make sure we carry our symbol of Jesus's victory over darkness with us everywhere, every day we are alive on this earth. Let's commit together to run our race set before us with purpose and endurance.

> *Therefore we also, since we are surrounded by so great a cloud of witnesses, let us lay aside every weight, and the sin*

which so easily ensnares us, and let us run with endurance the race that is set before us.

                                                  Hebrews 12:1 (NKJV)

SUFFERING

For our light and momentary troubles are achieving for us an eternal glory that far outweighs them all.

                                                  2 Corinthians 4:17(NLT)

The life of a warrior for Jesus is one of suffering. But like the passages above shows us, our suffering as Christians is on purpose. We have to embrace it, and like so many before us, find joy in it, and never forget this world is not our home.

This message was ingrained into my head when we stopped to tour an ancient church when I was on a mission trip in Armenia. As we hiked up to this beautiful church I had no idea about the life of Saint Gregory, and honestly I really didn't even know why we were stopping other than the church was beautiful. When we made it to the top of the climb, we sat together and listened to one of our missionaries share the story of why we were there. There was this man with a passion on his heart to bring the message of the cross to this area. He traveled out to the region we were in before 300 A.D. He eventually was punished for sharing his faith in this land. The King sentenced him to live in a cave about 25-30 feet deep with one small hole in the top and no end date. This was by all means a death sentence by starvation and isolation. This man, Saint Gregory lived in this cave for 13 years! There was a lady that would come and drop food in the cave to feed him and that nourishment was just enough to keep him alive, along with his unwavering faith in Jesus. After 13 years the King become extremely ill. He called for his magicians and healers and nobody could help him. Someone reminded him of this Christian, Gregory, so he called him out of the cave. Saint Gregory stood before the King, prayed for his healing and the Lord moved. The King was so awe stuck by this Gregory's God, that he made his nation a Christian nation. This was in 301 A.D. and this became the first Christian nation. Praise God!

After hearing about Saint Gregory's story and going down in the cave, my perspective of suffering for Jesus changed. There are so many times I complain about "suffering" when it's just a minor inconvenience. Saint Gregory's life inspired me more than ever to be all in for Jesus. To pray and ask Him to use me, no matter what that means. And when we pray like that, the selfless prayer that doesn't fear death and being shamed for our faith, we stand on the same ground of incredible saints that have come before us.

COURAGE

I want us to take a look at a modern day saint, and hands down the most passionate woman I have ever met for evangelizing the message of the cross. This story also comes from a mission trip I went on. And I have to say, if you have never been on a short term mission trip, please start praying for the Lord to lead your heart to the right trip for you. I believe short term missions trips are some of the most transformational experiences in the life of a believer.

I want to set the scene for this story. This was our third day of sharing the hope, forgiveness and love of Jesus with people in this country. Our team had prepared themselves with prayer, and we were with an incredible mission team serving on the site there. The day started off great. We were sharing the Gospel with people, walking through the villages and engaging in incredible conversations with people all day long about the Lord. I was feeling pretty exhausted toward the end of the day. As we were driving to pick up the other people on our team and make our hour drive back to the church, we pulled up to pick up a group with one of the female missionaries living in this country. She was already dealing with some spiritual warfare with her health, she had recently gotten out of the hospital for losing a lot of weight too fast, but she was serving Jesus with all of her strength. Truly an inspiring woman...

As we opened the door I heard her coughing... I looked around and the town was burning their grass in the ditches, smoke was rising everywhere. It hit me, she was having an asthma attack and we were in a van without air conditioning (air conditioning helps keep the outside air out). We got her in the car and got out of there. We had to leave some of our team behind at this point. I taught CPR and First Aid in the military for three and a half years and I knew this situation wasn't good. This little woman started going through a fight for her life. We sped out of there, as she was coughing hard and not getting much oxygen in her lungs. Her condition started to go down hill fast. The inhaler wasn't strong enough to help, I knew we needed to act. Everyone in the car started to pray out loud...and not weak prayers; these were life and death prayers. I took my sweatshirt off, put water on it and had her hold it over her mouth to moisten the air she was breathing, but the progress wasn't fast enough. We stopped at a gas station to see if we could get her in an air conditioned room while we tried to flag down a car with air conditioning to drive her the rest of the 45 minutes to town. She was so weak I had to run and carry her inside. We were asking people to drive her and no one was responding, so we had to risk it. We put her back in the car and drove as fast as possible to where she was staying. I have been with some incredible drivers, but this soldier of Jesus who was driving was driving like a pro! He was flying because we all knew there was a war for her life. We were warring in the Spirit for her and we weren't going to let satan take the life of this woman of faith without a fight. We all worked together to keep her alive and calm, even though I knew she could very well die. I sat holding this little woman's back with my left hand making sure her lungs were moving, holding a wet sweater to her face with her head tilted back because she was too weak to hold up her arms. I was speaking faith into her life even though fear was screaming in my ears, but I was speaking calm faith filled words in her ears. I just kept thinking, this is what living as a sacrifice for God looks like. She knew her health risks, but she was on the field anyway. She was not living in excuses, but was making the decision to live as a sacrifice of service for God's Glory. We eventually made it back to her apartment and got her hooked up on her nebulizer. She was weak and what her body went through was horrible, but praise God she made it out alive.

Now I had been working in fitness for a while at this time, and I knew what she just went through was one of the most physically demanding things the human body can go through. Our team got her back to her apartment late, and her husband and children cared for her as we went back to where we were staying. I knew we had an early morning the next morning, with a long day of ministry ahead... I thought there was no way she could make it.

The next morning as our team was getting ready to go, this little woman came walking through the door, tears in her eyes and a smile on her face. She was ready to go serve Jesus. She understood more than anyone I have been around that our suffering as followers of Jesus is inevitable, but it cannot stop us. She spent that entire day in pain, but nobody would have known it. She was focused on sharing Jesus and building relationships. We have to keep that same focus. The message of the cross is too important to let suffering keep us from sharing the Good News with others because of our physical suffering.

After the mission trip this woman sent me such a kind email about our trip. And here's what she ended her email with, and it still rings in my ears…I pray it never stops ringing in yours.

Let's leave it all on the field! Let's be poured out like a drink offering. Let's work until He comes.

THE FORK

But put on the Lord Jesus Christ, and make no provision for the flesh, to fulfill its lusts.

Romans 13:14 (NKJV)

After spending time focusing on the most powerful weapon on this earth for the Kingdom of God, the cross, we now have to study the greatest weapon on earth for the kingdom of darkness, the fork that feeds our flesh. As warriors for Jesus on this earth, by His grace and strength, we have to study and know our enemy. We cannot think for one minute that satan and his demons aren't waiting to devour us. He is waiting and ready to launch an attack against anyone who advances the Gospel. The last thing satan wants is for men to live courageously for Jesus by carrying our cross daily and sharing about the power of the resurrected cross. Satan wants to see men overlooking the importance of loving Jesus wholly, loving their wives like Christ, training their children up in the Lord, and evangelizing the Good News of Jesus Christ daily. There are so many areas where satan and his demons will sidetrack us in this life so we don't pursue these most important things daily. What are some of these sidetracks? From loving football, to being overly committed to our careers, to ignoring the health of our bodies, to watching a little porn here and there describes just a few of the sidetracks we can find ourselves on. I truly believe there is a war every morning of our lives to pursue anything other than loving Jesus and loving others like Jesus.

> I say then: Walk in the Spirit, and you shall not fulfill the lust of the flesh. For the flesh lusts against the Spirit, and the Spirit against the flesh; and these are contrary to one another, so that you do not do the things that you wish.
> Galatians 5:16-17 (NKJV)

This is a war for us to choose between feeding the Spirit by picking up our cross daily or the fork that feeds our flesh. And the choice of picking up our cross leads to life in Jesus and the desires of our flesh being crucified.

The only power we have as Christians is found in the Spirit filled life, which means being humble and broken before the Lord, knowing we cannot do anything good on our own-and this is what the cross of Jesus signifies. Knowing without the power of the cross we would be nothing, and have nothing, but with the cross...watch out! With the cross we have our forgiveness, our salvation through the shedding of the blood of Jesus, we have the resurrection power of Jesus, and we have the filling of the Holy Spirit. But there is an incredible battle for us to live every day knowing the power of the cross. There is a constant battle for us to not pick up our cross and choose the delicacies of what the fork that feeds our flesh has to offer.

And our lives are shaped by that daily decision...

> Do not be deceived, God is not mocked; for whatever a man sows, that he will also reap. For he who sows to his flesh will of the flesh reap corruption, but he who sows to the Spirit will of the Spirit reap everlasting life.
> Galatians 6:7-8 (NKJV)

When we use the fork of our flesh it leads to feeding something that should never be alive in our lives, and we slowly start to hide that area of our lives by covering it with a "mask." And that masked area causes our lives to slowly destruct, one fork size bite at a time. Satan's greatest desire is for you to become numb to the fork size bites with which you're feeding your flesh with, because he knows when we do that it will nourish and give strength to the sin in our lives. And satan knows when we feed sin bite by bite it will grow in power and strength, and he knows the outcome of that in a man's life. We have to remember satan is smarter than we will ever be, he knows the nature of a man and our temptations better than we ever will. He knows God's unconditional love for humans better than we ever will, and he hates it. It's the thing satan doesn't want anyone to ever hear, and he will try to kill anyone that forcefully advances the message of God's unconditional love. And he isn't going to kill us by coming into our house at night as a scary goblin. He is going to use the small, daily fork size bites to kill us. It is crucial that we become aware of this strategic attack on our lives, and put a stop to it by putting our fork down and picking up our cross each morning.

The thief's purpose is to steal and kill and destroy. My purpose is to give them a rich and satisfying life.

John 10:10 (NLT)

THE FORK AND OUR CAREERS

If you're like me, this is a major struggle. I would have to say I struggle with this weekly, and I have an accountability partner help keep me in check here. As men our flesh finds thrill in the chase, in the hunt. If we're not careful, in our careers the chases and hunts can become addicting, one fork bite at a time. Put yourself in the moment…

You come home from a busy day, you know you're supposed to engage with your family but you can't stop thinking about that project at work. You are challenged by that project, you're in the hunt for finishing the project well and you're slowly becoming a slave to the project. Don't act like it hasn't happened. Have you ever been sitting at the dinner table with your wife, and you bring up your day and the project you are on and she isn't interested at all? She wants to talk about the projects you are overlooking around the house, like dishes, vacuuming, dusting, etc. She might even bring those projects up, maybe with a comment like this, "I wish you would use that same energy you have for your career here in the house." Ouch! We have to remember as men we are wired differently. This is a common area we struggle with, but we cannot accept failure. We cannot justify feeding the hungers of our flesh in the area of our career.

I have good news though! God made you to be wired like you are, but He also sent His Son to die on the cross for us because He knew we cannot do anything good on our own. So God wants you to lean on Him for strength, and not be controlled by anything other than His Spirit. He wants us to be His bondservants, not bondservants to our careers. So work hard during the day, but when it's family time, be there 100%. I know it's hard, but join in the struggle with the rest of us; because there is more life in what God desires for you than any desire you can have outside of God's will.

THE FORK AND OUR HEALTH

Don't you realize that your body is the temple of the Holy Spirit, who lives in you and was given to you by God? You do not belong to yourself, for God bought you with a high price. So you must honor God with your body.
1 Corinthians 6:19-20 (NLT)

Men, we have to take a stand here, it is not an option. The obesity epidemic in this world today is greater than we have seen in our lives, and it is killing more people than ever before. This book is written to the men with the warrior hearts, we have to use that passion with our health. If you're reading this and you don't struggle with your weight you're not off the hook. The human body either gets healthier or unhealthier. So if you're not actively progressing with your health, your health is digressing. And satan wants to see your health poor because then you won't have the energy to:

Go into all the world and preach the gospel to every creature.
Mark 16:15 (NKJV)

Your wife, your kids, and this world need you to lead in this area. If you don't who will? We live in a hurting world that needs Christians to have energetic bodies that are ready for war. Ready to get in the fight and love and serve people like Jesus, and who are ready to walk with people through the hard times of life, sharing the hope and love of Jesus.

I could cover all of the statistics with you, but we all know obesity and a sedentary lifestyle are dangerous problems. I personally believe the health of our bodies is one of satan's biggest attacks on the life of the committed Christian. If we were a part of a special forces team for this country and we are so heavy we can't go for our morning run, we would have a problem. The focus of the physical training for a special forces group isn't just the running, it's running to train their mind, heart and body for the stresses of war. Special forces groups run so much and strive to have lean bodies because they want to be able to perform the best they can when the war is waging on their mission and the stress levels are the highest. We have men giving their lives to be the elite for the freedom of this country, and praise God for those soldiers! But God's Army needs men to be ready to lay down their lives for the eternal freedom that was bought for us on the cross. So lock your mind in, make the commitment today that your health will never be overlooked again. Please, make the commitment with me to live as elite soldiers of God with your body, soul and spirit. Never forget this is a commitment that can only be done when we pick up our cross daily and yield our bodies to the power of the Holy Spirit living inside of us. If you made this commitment with me, please understand your flesh is going to be ready to wage war with your new commitment. And the only way to win in a war with our flesh is by putting down the fork that feeds it every morning, and picking up our cross daily.

Therefore, brethren, we are debtors—not to the flesh, to live according to the flesh. For if you live according to the flesh you will die; but if by the Spirit you put to death the deeds of the body, you will live.
Romans 8:12-13 (NKJV)

Feeding our flesh is like feeding a baby lion in a secret room in our inner lives with fork size bites. At first the little lion is cute and friendly, then we keep feeding it, bite by bite and the lion grows stronger. One day we walk in with our fork to feed this lion, and we see it's fully-grown and ready to eat more than one bite of our fork. It wants our lives, and suddenly the lion attacks us and completely destroys us because of the nourishment we have given it, one bite at a time over a long period.

Taking that example, if you feed your flesh a little bite here, a little bite there, all of the sudden you're 100 pounds away from your ideal weight and your heart is struggling to make it to tomorrow. Our only hope with gaining victory over the delicious bites of the fork, is by finding our delight in the Lord. Our fork needs to be laid down at the foot of the cross every morning. We have to choose carrying the cross over eating from our fork that feeds our flesh. Remember we're in this together, but like the Navy SEALs say, "the only easy day was yesterday." So don't think it will ever get easier to lay the fork that feeds your flesh down, it will always be difficult, but it will always be rewarding when we do it. The flesh will always desire instant gratification without thinking of the consequence, where the Holy Spirit always thinks about the consequence of the seed we are sowing into our lives. Throughout this challenge we will experience this together, and Hell Week will help us all identify the voice of the flesh clearer than ever before…it's going to be a blast! Here's to living elite for Jesus!

> You've all been to the stadium and seen the athletes race. Everyone runs; one wins. Run to win. All good athletes train hard. They do it for a gold medal that tarnishes and fades. You're after one that's gold eternally. I don't know about you, but I'm running hard for the finish line. I'm giving it everything I've got. No sloppy living for me! I'm staying alert and in top condition. I'm not going to get caught napping, telling everyone else all about it and then missing out myself.
> 1 Corinthians 9:24-27 (The Message)

THE FORK AND OUR EVANGELISM

The fork that feeds our flesh is the worst enemy of evangelism. If we are feeding our sinful nature, we are slowly becoming disconnected from the sweet brokenness of a man that loves Jesus with everything he is. When we get disconnected from the Spirit of God by focusing on the appetites of the flesh, our eyes get blinded to the spiritual needs and activity around us. Evangelism should be one of the main focuses of every born again child of God, and evangelism only becomes a need in our lives when we have our daily focus on the cross. One of my biggest fears is not acting on the opportunity to share the Good News that saved me from hell after I leave this earth, and from the hell I was living in on this earth.

I was recently on a mission trip to Armenia and the Lord allowed me to see the importance of evangelism in so many ways. Over the 10 day trip, with seven days on the ground there our team of five saw 23 people repent and receive Jesus as their Savior. Praise God! It was amazing to see what happens when a team prays, and then acts on their faith. We went into villages just walking and praying for the Lord to lead us to the right people, and He would. God is so faithful. We were so focused and so bold for the Lord during that trip, and that was the first time in my life I witnessed a whole household surrender their life to Jesus for the first time. Truly amazing! We also established some incredible relationships with leaders of schools in the towns to get fitness evangelists in their system with the hope of sharing the love of Jesus with them. But one thing stood out to me the most, and I want to share that story with you.

One night our team was sitting down for dinner after a great day of evangelism in the surrounding villages. Over this dinner the pastor of the local church shared his testimony with us, and I will forever be changed…

This pastor told about growing up in the Soviet Union and having a father that was a very influential man in that time. His father died when this pastor was a young man, leaving him to be the man of the house before the age of 10. With the level of influence his father had, there was a pressure for this young man to fill his shoes. So he started down that path. He told us that he had looked for love and acceptance and he found it from his 35-40 year old friends when he was a teenager. As he was sharing with us he was showing us the scars on his hands from the knife fights he got into as he was the leader of a gang of 100 tough people in the Soviet Union. He was known as a fearless fighter and leader, he said he really wasn't afraid of anyone. One night he was walking through what is downtown Armenia now, and someone handed him a tract. He couldn't see the person's face, but they handed him the tract and he took it. He took the tract home and looked at it. On the front was a picture of a road that split in two at one point. One arrow leading to hell and the other to heaven. He knew for the first time he was going down the wrong path. He read the tract and couldn't get it out of his mind. The next day, he felt something in him urging him to go back downtown. He wasn't sure why, he had never experienced anything like that before. For him downtown was a long trip from where he was, but the feeling was so strong he left and went downtown. When he was walking around he noticed a young man preaching in the open air. He said there were about 40 people standing around the man listening, so he stayed back just far enough where he could hear. He was amazed, it was like this man was speaking directly to him. His heart grew extremely heavy, and all of the sudden this man started walking towards him. This man preaching lead him, a young gang leader, to the Lord that day, and he is now leading an incredible evangelistic church in Armenia. Praise God!

What's extremely intriguing about this encounter is that this Christian man with the tract who was evangelizing downtown was actually on a vacation from Canada. This man felt guilty that he was spending all of his vacation enjoying himself and wasn't sharing the Gospel. So he decided to go out one night and pass out tracts on the corner of a street in downtown and preach in open air the next morning. Talk about a warrior for Jesus… But with the work this man did for the Lord, there was only one person who repented in his efforts. That one person was on a path to Hell, heard the message of the cross, repented, and he has been serving Jesus passionately since then and has led so many people to the Lord Jesus.

So men, we have a responsibility… No matter if one person accepts Jesus as Lord or one thousand. There are so many people living around us right now that don't know Jesus, who will die and go to Hell if we don't tell them. The best thing we could ever do for another person is share the message of the cross of Jesus with them. We have to break the silence in this world, we have to live everyday unashamed of the Gospel, this world needs to hear about Jesus!

Lord, give me firmness without hardness, steadfastness without dogmatism, love without weakness.

Jim Elliot

THE SOULCON DESCRIPTION

SOULCON is an acronym I made that's short for soul control. This is the lifestyle I desire for all of us men to live. A lifestyle of submitting the control of our mind, will and emotions (our soul) to the Holy Spirit on a daily basis with the focus of special forces soldiers of Jesus. This is the process of dying to yourself and developing your spiritual man as you walk controlled by the Holy Spirit. I personally believe if we can all live a SOULCON lifestyle the obesity epidemic would stop in the church, and men would starve the appetites of their flesh on all levels because the men would finally be turning to the cross of Jesus instead of using their fork to feed areas of their flesh. The fork and the cross are two powerful tools and we have to choose what tool we are going to use daily. I don't know about you, but I want my death song to be valiant. I don't want people saying at my funeral that he was a good man but he just couldn't stop overeating, or he was a good man but his porn addiction tore apart his family and ruined his impact with his kids and caused his wife to leave him, or his anger got the best of him in that traffic jam and the wrong person was on the other side of his anger that time, or he fed his desire to be a workaholic and unfortunately missed out on his kids growing up and he never was really close with his kids during the most important time. I pray for all of us that these things are never said. I pray we make the necessary changes during this six-week challenge to live life under the control of the Holy Spirit because we all know His control is so much better than the control of our own flesh. Over this challenge the readings are broken down into daily devotionals of a fictional journey where we will cover, in my opinion, the essentials for you to live the rest of your life as a special forces soldier for Jesus. In this fictional journey you will learn more about who you are in Christ and what He has in store for men that truly seek and follow Him. I'm so pumped! Allow your imagination to soar and have fun with it. But first, I want you to take a few minutes and read through these four fundamentals. Don't skim over them, they are crucial to your understanding of some of the physical challenges you will be putting your body through over the next six weeks.

After the fundamentals I have the six-week objectives, and then we will get started!

THE 4 FUNDAMENTALS OF THE SOULCON CHALLENGE

When making the switch to a SOULCON lifestyle there are four main fundamentals that need to be a part of your daily routine. Just like in basketball or other sports, the fundamentals are something that the athletes learn in the beginning but they will use them to fine-tune their success for the rest of their careers. The fundamentals of SOULCON will cover:

- What you drink
- What you eat
- Exercise
- Rest

If you learn and apply theses fundamentals properly, they will eventually become quality habits that will be as natural to you as dribbling a basketball is to a professional basketball player.

Before we dive into the first fundamental, there's one thing that I want to take time to clarify that will hopefully clear up some confusion.

There are two different types of carbohydrates: simple and complex. I am sure you have heard these terms, but I want to take a moment to clarify the difference between the two. Once we do this, learning and being able to apply the fundamentals will be much easier. There are also a few other simple items I want to explain before you start. Just think of this as a basic nutrition 101 course.

Simple Carbohydrates
These are the carbohydrates that truly inhibit a SOULCON lifestyle. These carbohydrates are sugars, white breads, white rice, white pasta, sodas, concentrated fruit juices, candy, sugary baked goods, doughnuts, and the list goes on.

I want you to look at these types of carbohydrates as a simple math problem, like 2+2, and your body as the problem solver. Your body looks at these types of carbohydrates as easy problems to solve, and quickly solves the 2+2 problem, and releases the energy into your system. This is a very harmful thing that inhibits losing body-fat because the faster carbohydrates digest, the more likely it will be stored as body-fat. Your body only needs a certain amount of energy at one time, and when you exceed that amount; your body sends all of the extra energy remaining in your bloodstream into your body-fat stores. This is why there is a need to send a more complex, challenging math problem into your system.

Complex Carbohydrates
These are the carbohydrates that you want to have as part of your daily diet. These carbohydrates are sweet potatoes, brown rice, oatmeal, 100% whole-wheat bread, whole wheat pasta, couscous, quinoa, etc.

When you think of, or hear me talk about complex carbohydrates, I want you to think of this like a long division problem that your body (the problem solver) has to solve out by hand. The longer your body (the problem solver) takes to solve the problem (digest the energy), the less likely that you will be able to store energy as body fat. Complex carbohydrates are great because they contain fiber, which causes the body to break down the energy slowly, giving you sustained energy until your next meal.

Lean Protein
The United States Department of Agriculture defines lean meat as having less than 10 grams of total fat, 4.5 grams or less of saturated fat and fewer than 95 milligrams of cholesterol in a 3.5-ounce portion. Here are some great sources for lean protein:

- White meat from chicken and turkey
- Fish provides lean protein along with omega-3 fatty acids that lower cholesterol and inhibit inflammation
- Red meat including cuts like: sirloin, flank steak, rump roast, top loin, top round and extra lean ground beef
- Pork center loin and tenderloin
- Low-fat dairy products also qualify as sources of lean protein
- Quinoa is a low-fat grain that's a complete protein
- Beans and legumes are naturally low-fat sources of protein

Fats

Contrary to the popular belief in the early 90's fats are crucial for the health of your body, we just need to make sure we are fueling our bodies with the healthy fats and staying clear of the unhealthy fats. There are four different types of fats in the foods we consume: trans fats (extremely dangerous), saturated fats (dangerous), monounsaturated fats (healthy) and polyunsaturated fats (extremely healthy). The dangerous fats, saturated and trans fats, tend to be more solid at room temperature (like a stick of butter), while the healthy fats, monounsaturated and polyunsaturated fats tend to be more liquid (like olive oil). The dangerous fats, saturated fats and trans fats raise bad cholesterol (LDL) levels in your blood. The healthy fats, monounsaturated and polyunsaturated fats can lower bad cholesterol levels and are extremely beneficial to your health when consumed on a daily basis. Just know one gram of fat yields nine calories, so even though the healthy fats are incredible for your body, the calories can add up quickly. So enjoy them, understand your body needs them for fuel and just don't go overboard. This journey to optimal health is about living each day in self-control and fueling your body properly.

Fruits and Vegetables

The American Heart Association recommends eating eight or more fruit and vegetable servings every day. An average adult consuming 2,000 calories daily should aim for 4.5 cups of fruits and vegetables a day. All of our daily diets need more fruits and veggies. These are additions to our diets that will increase our productivity and help fuel our bodies to carry out the mission God gave us with the highest amount of health possible. You might have questions about organic vs. nonorganic, but just focus on consuming fruits and vegetables to start. Wash them thoroughly, and then get them in your system. Once you develop the habit of consuming the recommended amount of fruits and vegetables, then you can research further if organic or nonorganic is the fit for your lifestyle. Just do your best and spread out your fruits and veggies throughout the day. Focus on having balanced, colorful meals.

Hopefully this has given you a foundational understanding of nutrition along with understanding some key terminology. We will now dive into the four fundamentals of healthy living that I have put together and used to help people transform their health for over a decade.

No matter where you are, or what your budget is, you can live a SOULCON lifestyle. I just want to encourage you to not be intimidated and to remember that a car that is in motion is a lot easier to drive than a car that's parked. So let's get rolling...

FUNDAMENTAL 1
— WHAT YOU DRINK

> *So whether you eat or drink, or whatever you do, do it all for the glory of God.*
> 1 Corinthians 10:31 (NLT)

Now that we have our foundation, let's dive into the first fundamental, what you drink.

This can be the silent killer of any healthy lifestyle, whether your goal is to gain lean body mass or lose body fat. This fundamental should be something that everyone is aware of, and one everyone should take the time to learn the proper "technique." Remember, our goal is to make this as simple as possible so you can start practicing these fundamentals and turn them into a lifestyle.

One of the most important things for everyone to understand is water is the best thing you can drink ... period. I recommend for everyone to drink at least 64 ounces of water per day; however ½ your bodyweight in ounces of water per day would be optimal! Here is some information to help you understand the importance of drinking water daily:
- Your body is about 70% water
- Your muscles are about 75% water
- Your brain cells are about 85% water
- Your blood is approximately 82% water
- Even your bones are approximately 25% water
- Water is the main lubricant in the joint spaces and helps prevent arthritis and back pain
- Water increases the efficiency of the immune system
- Water prevents the clogging of arteries in the heart and brain, and thus helps reduce the risk of heart attack and stroke

- Water helps prevent memory loss as we age, reducing the risk of degenerative diseases such as Alzheimer's disease, multiple sclerosis, Parkinson's disease, and Lou Gehrig's disease
- Water affects our appearance, making our skin smoother and giving it sparkling luster; it also reduces the effects of aging

Tip: Carry a water bottle around with you throughout the day. This is a great way to measure your water intake and make sure you get at least 64 ounces a day.

Coffee and Teas

Contrary to popular belief, coffee is actually extremely healthy for your body. One 8 ounce cup of black coffee (without cream and sugar) is full of antioxidants (molecules that may protect cells from the damage caused by unstable molecules known as free radicals) for your body. There has been plenty of research to show that coffee can be a great addition to a healthy diet.

Remember too much of a good thing can be bad. If you have too many cups of coffee it will have a negative effect on your day. I recommend for you to stay below six 8 ounce cups of coffee per day. There are certain cases where your current health condition won't allow you to drink coffee, but for the average person without a condition noted from their doctor, coffee is a great healthy addition to your diet. I absolutely love starting my mornings off with coffee, and want to encourage you to do the same.

As for teas, they also have a healthy component. Black, unsweetened tea has high levels of antioxidants and can be a beneficial beverage in your diet. Green, white, and herbal teas all have similar benefits for your body and can be highly beneficial. I hope that you will implement different types of teas into your daily routine along with healthy eating.

Regular and Diet Soda

If you are a person that has a regular soda on a daily basis, I plead with you to stop. Aside from the negative effects that drinking soda has on your teeth, it is making your body more susceptible to Type 2 Diabetes and numerous other diseases.

I want to encourage you, if you like soda to enjoy a soda on your rest day (we will learn about this in fundamental four), but other than that this is one of those things that are best left untouched.

There is nothing positive about soda; all of the effects on your body are negative. I have written these fundamentals to help you live life as healthy as possible so you can have the energy to serve Christ joyfully the rest of your life. I hope and pray this is your goal, and making the decision to quit drinking soda will help you tremendously.

What about diet soda? There are numerous different ideas and research out there on diet soda. The truth is, it is not beneficial for your body either. The chemical sweetener aspartame IS dangerous to your overall health. However, if you are a person that has to have soda on a daily basis, it is my opinion that diet soda is the lesser of the two evils. Do your best to limit your intake of diet soda, and focus on drinking things that will help improve your health.

Sports Drinks
Are sports drinks beneficial? For a small majority of people they are very beneficial. These groups include high endurance athletes, bodybuilders and people that workout for longer than 60 minutes. No matter what your goals are, your body responds the same way when you consume sugary drinks throughout the day. Sugar signals to your body to increase its insulin levels when it is flooded with the fast digesting sugar (simple carbohydrate) you just ingested. This increase of glucose (sugar) in your blood will likely be more energy than your body needs for the given time, which will cause your liver to store the excess energy as body fat. This is something you want to stay away from, since you are on your journey to optimal health. During the day instead of grabbing a sugary sports drink, grab something with little to no sugars, ideally water, but some great options are: G2, Propel, and other flavored waters with little to no calories.
Of course, the list above is not all inclusive. However, I wanted to list some of the most common beverages that we as humans consume on a daily basis. I want to encourage you to do some research on your own and use the foundation you have from these fundamentals to see if the beverages you consume are beneficial or not for your daily diet. I am a major advocate of taking ownership

of your nutrition and fitness, and being proactive in finding healthy alternatives.

Check below for other great alternatives, and make sure to check out the SOULCON App for more options and meal plans.

- Choose unsweetened tea rather than sweet tea. If you love sweet tea (like me) put 1-2 packets of stevia or truvia in your unsweetened tea.
- Choose skim milk over whole milk. The only difference between the two is the milk fat. Whole milk does not have more vitamins, minerals, or protein… Only more calories and fat.
- Choose skim milk over half and half in your coffee.
- Choose regular black coffee over an energy drink. Most energy drinks have WAY too much caffeine and will have an adverse effect on your body's long term energy levels. Yes, coffee does have caffeine but not in excess and it also provides powerful antioxidants which provide many health benefits. Remember that too much of a good thing is still bad.
- Skim milk, soy milk, almond milk and Greek yogurt based smoothies over non-fat frozen yogurt or sherbet smoothies–not all smoothies are healthy. Some smoothies can be full of sugar. Ensure that the smoothie you are making or purchasing is made with real fruit (fresh or frozen) and if juice is used, make sure it's 100% fruit juice and not just sugary syrup.

FUNDAMENTAL 2
— WHAT YOU EAT

Subdue your appetites, my dears, and you've conquered human nature.

Charles Dickens

The second fundamental is something we all do on a daily basis: eat. I have seen and heard some CRAZY diets, and I'm sure you have too. There are so many weight-loss pills, liquid diets, and low-carb diets that promise quick results but can be extremely dangerous and never attack the true issue: changing lifestyle habits. I am sure that many of you are or have been frustrated by the lack of clarity with some of these "fad" diets and are looking for something realistic that can get you your desired results. Well, I hope to encourage you and I want you to know wherever you are, and whatever your goals are, YOU can achieve them!

I'm not trying to sell you anything magic and I will never tell you that you will be able to get results without work. The truth is that your desired results are going to take hard work and discipline to reach them. I help everyone I work with realize the simplicity of proper nutrition and exercise, but I never tell them that the execution is easy. It is in the act of doing what you know is right that you run into the resistance of temptation. But with you and your SOULCON team, you are ready for the challenge! Just remember over this six-week journey the only easy day was the one before you started!

Breakfast

A commonly asked question is, "Do I need carbs if I'm trying to lose weight?" The simple answer is YES! The Lord made your body in a way that it needs carbohydrates (energy) in the morning to start the day. Do your best to choose complex carbohydrates (oatmeal, 100% whole wheat toast, low sugar cereal with >3g of fiber). I typically recommend between 20-50 grams of carbohydrates for breakfast. If you're not sure, check out the nutrition label or search for it on the internet. I am a major advocate of taking ownership and learning about the fuel we are putting in our bodies.

I recommend that you start every day by eating breakfast within 30-60 minutes of waking up, or after your morning workout. If you skip breakfast you will confuse your metabolism, and your body will not function at its highest level. If you miss breakfast too often you will slow your metabolism down, and your body will end up storing more energy during other meals. The more consistent you keep your metabolism the more energy you will have during the day, and the quicker you will get to your optimal weight.

Breakfast Options
- A healthy bowl of low sugar cereal with >3 grams of fiber, with skim milk, soy milk or almond milk and a piece of fruit
- One packet of lower sugar oatmeal with one whole egg and

two egg whites and a piece of fruit
- Two pieces of 100% whole wheat toast with one tablespoon of all natural peanut butter and a piece of fruit
- A meal replacement bar with around 15-20g of protein and a piece of fruit
- A meal replacement shake with 20-30g of whey protein (be aware of the sugar content as some of these are loaded with unnecessary sugar) and a piece of fruit

Snack

Ideally you should consume a snack consisting of complex carbohydrates and lean protein every 2-3 hours. This will not only allow adequate time for digestion between meals but also keep your blood sugar levels stable, thus increasing your metabolic rate. Your snack options should be between 150-200 calories. This will help satisfy your hunger and keep your body on course to living in optimal health.

Snack Options

- 15-30g of protein in a low carbohydrate protein shake made with water, skim milk, soy milk, almond milk or Greek yogurt
- An apple, pear, orange or grapefruit and a serving of unsalted nuts or two tablespoons of natural peanut butter
- A meal replacement bar with around 15-30g of protein and lower carbohydrates
- 100 calories almond pack and a piece of fruit
- Cottage cheese and fruit
- Mixed berries and Greek yogurt

Lunch

Your body needs some complex carbohydrates (energy) to fuel the rest of the day and it needs protein to help rebuild the muscles in your body that are being broken down, and it needs fruits and vegetables for antioxidants, vitamins, minerals and nutrients. Here are three easy steps to creating a healthy lunch:

- Fruits and veggies
- Complex carbohydrates
- Protein

Remember that if you provide your body with the right types of food at the right time it will start releasing the excess energy (body fat) it doesn't need. In short, in order to lose weight and decrease body fat, you must eat. It is about eating the right foods at the right time in the right amounts.

Lunch Options

- One sandwich, soup and an apple, try to use 100% whole wheat bread, with low calorie condiments and lean meat.
- Four to five ounces of lean meat on a salad, with unsalted nuts and fruit with low-fat/low-calorie dressing. (Best options: light vinaigrette, light Italian, olive oil and vinegar. Try to avoid low fat or fat-free ranch) and a sweet potato.
- Turkey burger with 100% whole wheat bun and a piece of fruit or small fruit bowl.

Snack

For this challenge you will cut out carbohydrates from grains and breads after 3pm (the only exceptions are sweet potatoes, vegetables, and berries). When you remove these carbohydrates from your diet after 3pm your body will still need energy and it will find it somewhere in your body, thus going into the energy storage that it has made (your body-fat). This is a great thing, and something that you want to happen! This will also help you identify hunger feelings from your flesh so you can work on feeding on God's Word instead of using your fork to quiet your flesh. This is one of the hardest things you will do with your body, but one of the most effective. Remember, we don't want easy, we want effective!

Snack Options:

- One to two handfuls of healthy nuts without salt and an apple, banana, or orange
- 20-30g of protein in a low carbohydrate protein shake made with water, soy milk, skim milk, almond milk or Greek yogurt
- One serving of cottage cheese and a piece of fruit
- Raw veggies with natural peanut butter or nut butter

Dinner

God has designed your body to rebuild itself at night while you are sleeping, and your body requires lean protein and healthy fat to do this.

Your body doesn't need carbohydrates at this time unless you are a bodybuilder, marathon runner or sumo wrestler. Just remember any carbohydrate at dinner that doesn't get used (most all of them) will be stored as body-fat while you sleep. If you don't give your body carbohydrates at this time your body will find energy from the storage inside of your body to help rebuild your muscles, in essence you will be burning body-fat while you sleep! What wonderful news! This will also help you learn how to master the appetites of your flesh by leaning on the Spirit's help to not turn to carbs for comfort.

Dinner Options
(make sure you have at least one cup of veggies)
- Four to five ounces of lean meat, i.e. turkey breast, chicken breast, lean 93/7 ground beef, fish, etc. with veggies, veggies, veggies!!!! (Try to stick with steamers or fresh vegetables and get three different color of veggies with dinner)
- Salad topped with meat and nuts and with low-fat/low-calorie dressing. Best options: light vinaigrettes, light Italian, olive oil and vinegar (try and avoid low fat or fat-free ranch)

Let dinner be your last meal and do your best to not eat within two hours of going to bed.

Check out the meal plans, recipes, and workout plans on the SOULCON App. Just do your best to make healthy choices, and stay in control of your portion sizes.

Feast Days
For this challenge we will eat healthy six days during the week and have one day of feasting...after Hell Week. The lifestyle I encourage is healthy six days and feasting one day, but for the nature of this challenge, the first four weeks are clean eating, your first feast will be after Hell Week. This is something that I will cover in detail with the fourth fundamental, but that feast day will be one of your favorite days of this challenge, and as you continue to make SOULCON a lifestyle it will become one of your favorite days every week. God desires and has intended for you take one day per week and rest. This rest includes your strict exercise and eating plan.

FUNDAMENTAL 3
— EXERCISE

Do not let what you cannot do interfere with what you can do.
John Wooden

As we continue our journey through the 4 Fundamentals of Healthy Living, I hope you understand and look forward to implementing the first two fundamentals in your daily life. Just like anything in this life, it is easier to fill your life with good than to try to get rid of the bad. Focus on having more of the healthy options, and do your best not to dwell on the foods or drinks in which you are trying to eliminate. This is a concept that I hope you use in your daily walk with health as well as with the Lord.

Living healthy should be a very positive transition in your life, and your success in this transition will come from focusing your attitude on the positive changes. If you mope around all day thinking about foods that are harmful to your health like donuts, soda, or fried foods, you will be living a diet that will soon DIE off in your life. There has to be a paradigm shift in your mind that will allow you to look at healthy living in a whole new light.

I know there are a lot of negative connotations with living healthy and most people think it is too time consuming, too expensive, or that it is just not worth it! I hope through these four fundamentals, you come to a wonderful realization that living healthy is very rewarding and by changing your daily routine you will make a positive impact on your entire life. This brings us to the third fundamental, exercise.

Similar to the other two fundamentals we have discussed, there has to be a paradigm shift in your mind to understand the importance of having exercise as part of your daily routine. If you take one thing away from this section, remember the key to optimal health is to eat less and move more! In order to make exercise a part of your daily routine, let's focus on some of the benefits of exercise.

Exercise will:
- Help strengthen your heart
- Improve the strength of your muscles, bones and joints
- Burn calories

- Help you feel more vibrant, and better able to cope with stress
- Help you have better quality sleep

Exercise will reduce the risk of (although there are some genetic components that are the exception):
- Premature death from heart disease
- Developing diabetes
- Developing high cholesterol
- Developing high blood pressure
- Living with the negative side-effects of being obese

Hopefully with the benefits listed above, this will help motivate you to understand the importance of exercise and that the investment is worth the time. You need to believe that you are worth it! Start simple, to ensure that you can keep an exercise routine for the rest of your life. There will never be a place in your life when you no longer have to exercise. Exercise is something we as humans should do regularly to live a long, healthy life.

This is what I recommend for making exercise a part of your lifestyle. The best thing you can do is to K.I.S.S. (Keep It Simple Saint):
- Exercise with your heart rate between 60% and 85% of your maximum heart rate. The formula for your maximum heart rate is 220 minus (your age).
- Perform repetitions of 15-25 with a 0-15 second rest during your weight training sessions.
- Do your best to push yourself with each challenge in this book, with the hopes in makeing SOULCON a lifestlye.

Tip: Many times with exercise we can produce a lot of zeal at first, and convince ourselves that we can take on more than is realistically possible. When you feel comfortable or your schedule begins to allow for more time, increase your time spent exercising. This will minimize the feeling of discouragement and defeat by keeping your goals realistic and sets you up for greater success!

These are a few pointers to help start you in the right direction. I know that around 95% of the time you will not feel like exercising. Our hope is that you keep your eyes fixed on the benefits of exercise and not on the emotions that you feel before you start exercising.

There will come a day when you will enjoy the feeling after your workout enough that the (good) pain you go through during the workout will be totally worth it.

Make sure to check out the SOULCON App for sample workout plans for your specific goals.

FUNDAMENTAL 4
— REST

Rest is not idleness, and to lie sometimes on the grass under the trees on a summer's day, listening to the murmur of water, or watching the clouds float across the sky, is by no means a waste of time.

John Lubbock

As we come to the end of the 4 Fundamentals of the SOULCON Challenge, hopefully you have learned simple tools that can change your life. Just like in a sport, fundamentals are not things that you will learn once and then never use again. The fundamentals of healthy living are things that you will use the rest of your life, and you will keep fine-tuning. This brings us to the fourth fundamental: rest.

In our society today, I personally think that this is one of the most overlooked areas of healthy living. Is it healthy for your body to be working 24/7? Clearly the answer is no, but why do we try to fool ourselves? We all know numerous people who never slow down in life, they never truly rest.

The 4th Commandment
First, let's define what true rest is. True rest was shown to us by God when He took the seventh day off after creating the world in the previous six days. Did God need rest? Absolutely not, but He gave us an example of how to live.

When you read through the Old Testament, you will find a plethora of scriptures that cover taking one day of complete rest from work. This wasn't a cruel mandate by God to make humans less productive. God knew, as humans we need one day to recharge our brain, heart and muscular skeletal system. Jesus describes this in the New Testament in (Mark 2:27) by explaining the Sabbath was not created for God, but that God created it for us.

I want to challenge you to start taking one Sabbath day of rest per week. I know that this might seem impossible with your schedule, but it is absolutely crucial for the health of your soul and body. Do whatever you enjoy on this day, just do nothing that you would consider "work."

This is where I also recommend for you to take your rest from your healthy eating. Don't lose control and eat your house down, but allow yourself to enjoy the foods that you have been going without during the week. Delicious foods are a gift from God for us to enjoy in moderation, but it was never His intention for His creation to live a lifestyle of gluttony.

I desire that you apply this principle and you trust me that even with taking one full feast day per week in your SOULCON lifestyle (after Hell Week), you will still be able to hit your health and fitness goals. This is one thing that if you implement every week for the rest of your life, there is a good chance that it will affect the length of your life and I promise it will affect the quality of your life. I also promise you that by the time you hit those goals, you will be able to live that lifestyle for the rest of your life. I am not sharing something with you that is my own unique design; I'm sharing what I have found in the scriptures for God's children to be able to enjoy life.

A Good Night's Sleep

An area of rest we can practice on a daily basis and one that is essential to our bodies living in optimal health is sleep. If you are like most people, you probably don't have a caffeine deficiency, but more than likely you have a sleep deficiency. Our bodies were created to need sleep on a daily basis to be able to function at our highest level for the following day.

Most sleep studies have shown people who get less than 6 hours of sleep per night have their body signaling hunger incorrectly, throwing their hormones out of balance (as well as numerous other ill effects on our health). Our body has two main hormones that signal hunger: ghrelin, which signals our brain that we are hungry, and leptin, which signals to our brain that we are full. When we are not getting enough sleep the amount of ghrelin in our body increases and the amount of leptin decreases. What does this mean? This means that your body is hungrier more often throughout the day (high ghrelin levels) and that your body doesn't signal your brain when it's full (low leptin levels) when you are sleep deprived. Clearly this is something that we want to avoid as we continue in our journey of healthy living.

If you start by getting 6-8 hours of sleep per night this will help your body to equalize these hormone levels in your body, and better equip you to stay in control of the portion sizes that you consume throughout the day.

5 Practical Tips for a Good Night's Sleep

1. Control your sleep environment
   - Make your bedroom a safe place for sleep. Have a rule that there is no email or social media in your bedroom. These things can get your mind going, and that is a major inhibitor of a good night sleep. You want a peaceful mind when you lay down on the pillow. Sleep is important and we have to guard our environment to make sure we get the quantity and quality of sleep that we need to have the highest energy the next day.
   - If you are a TV watcher in bed, you might want to change. The light from the TV will increase your serotonin levels in your brain, and decrease your melatonin levels (serotonin is a feel good endorphin, and melatonin is a hormone that is crucial for a good night's sleep).
   - No snacking in bed. Eating carbohydrates too close to bed will also increase your serotonin levels and decrease your melatonin levels.
2. Keep a regular sleep cycle
   - Research reveals that the body operates on a 24-hour clock. This body clock is called circadian rhythms. Research reveals that for optimal functioning of mind and body, it is best to go to bed and wake up at the same time every day (including weekends).
3. Meditate on God's word
   - This is extremely important. Take 3-5 minutes before

bed and meditate on one of your favorite scriptures. Visualize the peace of the Lord, and how much He loves you. One of my favorites to meditate on before bed is Isaiah 26:3, "You will keep him in perfect peace, whose mind is stayed on You, because he trusts in You." (NKJV)

4. Exercise regularly
    *   When exercise is a part of your regular routine you will sleep better. When you lay down your body will be ready for rest. Exercise is still the only thing that will naturally lower and regulate your stress hormone (cortisol). When that hormone is elevated for too long, it will steal our much needed sleep from our lives.

5. Decrease your caffeine consumption
    *   If you consume caffeine too close to bed it will steal your much-needed sleep. Find what works best for you and your body.

THE SOULCON CHALLENGE

OVERVIEW

If you have specific nutritional needs or physical limitations, please consult with your physician before you start this challenge.

WEEK 01: TEST-IN WEEK
- Max Push-ups in 2 minutes
  - 2 minute rest
- Max Sit-ups in 2 minutes
  - 2 minute rest
- Run, walk, or crawl a 5k
  - Make sure to record your 5k time, push-up and sit-up count to challenge yourself on Week 6

WEEK 02: MAX WEEK
- Monday: Push-up day
  - You have 24 hours to do as many push-ups as possible
- Wednesday: Sit-up Day
  - You have 24 hours to do as many sit-ups as possible
- Friday: Bodyweight Squat Day
  - You have 24 hours to do as many squats as possible

WEEK 03: FAST WEEK
- Have one fast day with at least one person on your team.
  - On this day you will drink only water and black coffee.

WEEK 04: HELL WEEK (6 DAYS)
This week you are limited to fruit, veggies (including sweet potatoes, not white potatoes), lean proteins, unsalted nuts, and protein powders (no milk added, only water).

Also, there is no weight training this week, just daily push-ups and any bodyweight training you desire. Here's the challenge this week for you and your team:

(Push yourself as hard as possible, and have a healthy competition with the guys on your team)
- Miles from jogging or walking
- Miles from cycling
- Miles on the elliptical

WEEK 05: MAX WEEK # 2
- Monday: Push-up day
  - You have 24 hours to do as many push-ups as possible
- Wednesday: Sit-up Day
  - You have 24 hours to do as many sit-ups as possible
- Friday: Bodyweight Squat Day
  - You have 24 hours to do as many squats as possible

WEEK 06: TEST-OUT WEEK
- Max Push-ups in 2 minutes
  - 2 minute rest
- Max Sit-ups in 2 minutes
  - 2 minute rest
- Run, walk, or crawl a 5k

PRE CHALLENGE MOTIVATION

I want you to think back to your moment of salvation. The first time you met Jesus as your personal Savior. I want you to think of the emotions you felt, the weight that was lifted off of your life, and the unconditional love you experienced. That moment wasn't based on your personal performance as a good Christian, or a good person. That moment was a time when your faith was enough. Your faith in Jesus's sacrifice on the cross was stronger than your failures. We can never leave that sweet place. The people around us need to hear about that time, that moment when we accepted by faith, the sacrifice Jesus made for us. It's when we share the truth that the God of everything loves us at our worst, and helps us become our best that people start to hear the hope of Jesus.

If we feed our brain the message of the cross every morning, we are more aware of other's need for that message every day. If we feed our brain with pride, vanity or idols then we miss out on the opportunity to share the hope of the cross with hurting people around us. Trust me, I have lost focus so many times. I fail with this constantly, but I don't allow myself to become defined by those failures, and please, don't allow yourself to be identified by them either. As humans to fail is normal, experiencing distraction is normal, having terrible days is normal. We have to remember the cross is a symbol reminding us we could never be perfect. We have to remember this daily, and focus on Christ's performance being stronger than our own. When we do this we will have the strength to bounce back faster after we fall, and we will learn our focus on Christ and His love for us is the most powerful thing in our lives.

Picking up our cross and carrying it daily is our constant reminder that Jesus paid it all, He alone is our strength and life and our reminder that no matter what, we are willing to give Him every part of our lives.

The following of Christ is not the achievement or merit of a select few, but the divine commandment to all Christians without distinction.

Dietrich Bonhoeffer

Before you and your team of ideally 2-12 guys embark on this six-week challenge together, I want you to take a moment and read through the passage of scripture below. I fully believe it is in this text we find the daily battle to either pick up our cross or pick up our fork, and we find the ability to relate with one of the most elite special forces soldiers of God's army, the Apostle Paul. One of the key points I want to highlight in this passage is how our best day will never compare with Jesus's worst day, and that's why we need a Savior. We need the cross daily because it's the cross that reminds us Jesus our Savior had to come to earth as man (still 100% God), lived a sinless life, died a brutal death on a cross, and was resurrected from the dead so we could have the gift of the Holy Spirit living and dwelling in us. He did this because He loves us like crazy, and He knows we could never live a perfect day. So our call to be holy, to be perfect is one that is impossible on our own. It is impossible without the empty cross, without the power of the Holy Spirit in us. So remember as you go through this difficult journey, it's not about your perfection. It's about your focus on the One who is perfect, and stewarding these bodies to the best of your ability on this earth.

Now you may be like me at times and have the thought like, "why even try? If we could never be perfect or have a perfect day, then why not stay just like I am? I mean, God loves me like I am, and this challenge seems really difficult." I believe this is an extremely toxic thought from the enemy. As men, we cannot let the pain of failing along the way, or the pain of disappointment stop us from living in top physical, emotional and spiritual condition. Our family needs us to be as healthy as possible, our workplaces need it, and the world around us needs it. The healthier we are, the more strength we have to take the Good News of Jesus Christ into the dark areas of this earth. God knows we are human, He knows we have made and will continue to make mistakes, and He loves us unconditionally. He believes in us, and He wants to see us become trained in Him, to truly light up the world around us. Like special forces soldiers, we have to keep our eyes on the mission objectives, trained and ready for battle. In God's army, the most elite training is yielding to God's power daily and not the desires of our flesh. It is only then, when we are yielded and walking in the power of the Spirit, we can we carry out the mission objectives our Commander in Chief has given us. The following text is from Paul, one of the most elite soldiers God's army has ever seen. He shares the struggle of living in these bodies, and having the desire to please God. Please let this text ring in your thoughts throughout this challenge:

So the trouble is not with the law, for it is spiritual and good. The trouble is with me, for I am all too human, a slave to sin. I don't really understand myself, for I want to do what is right, but I don't do it. Instead, I do what I hate. But if I know that what I am doing is wrong, this shows that I agree that the law is good. So I am not the one doing wrong; it is sin living in me that does it.

And I know that nothing good lives in me, that is, in my sinful nature. I want to do what is right, but I can't. I want to do what is good, but I don't. I don't want to do what is wrong, but I do it anyway. But if I do what I don't want to do, I am not really the one doing wrong; it is sin living in me that does it.

I have discovered this principle of life—that when I want to do what is right, I inevitably do what is wrong. I love God's law with all my heart. But there is another power within me that is at war with my mind. This power makes me a slave to the sin that is still within me. Oh, what a miserable person I am! Who will free me from this life that is dominated by sin and death? Thank God! The answer is in Jesus Christ our Lord. So you see how it is: In my mind I really want to obey God's law, but because of my sinful nature I am a slave to sin.

So now there is no condemnation for those who belong to Christ Jesus. And because you belong to him, the power of the life-giving Spirit has freed you from the power of sin that leads to death. The law of Moses was unable to save us because of the weakness of our sinful nature. So God did what the law could not do. He sent his own Son in a body like the bodies we sinners have. And in that body God declared an end to sin's control over us by giving his Son as a sacrifice for our sins. He did this so that the just requirement of the law would be fully satisfied for us, who no longer follow our sinful nature but instead follow the Spirit.

Those who are dominated by the sinful nature think about sinful things, but those who are controlled by the Holy Spirit think about things that please the Spirit. So letting your sinful nature control your mind leads to death. But letting the Spirit control your mind leads to life and peace. For the sinful nature is always hostile to God. It never did obey God's laws, and it never will. That's why those who are still under the control of their sinful nature can never please God.

But you are not controlled by your sinful nature. You are controlled by the Spirit if you have the Spirit of God living in you. (And remember that those who do not have the Spirit of Christ living in them do not belong to him at all.) And Christ lives within you, so even though your body will die because of sin, the Spirit gives you life because you have been made right with God. The Spirit of God, who raised Jesus from the dead, lives in you. And just as God raised Christ Jesus from the dead, he will give life to your mortal bodies by this same Spirit living within you.

Therefore, dear brothers and sisters, you have no obligation to do what your sinful nature urges you to do. For if you live by its dictates, you will die. But if through the power of the Spirit you

*put to death the deeds of your sinful nature, you will live. For all
who are led by the Spirit of God are children of God.*

Romans 7:14-8:14 (NLT)

I challenge you to pray, right where you are and ask the Spirit to transform your mind, will and emotions during this challenge to understand this text. Ask the Spirit to help you learn the weakness of your flesh, and ask that He reveals how strong you are when you walk in Him daily.

These devotionals are meant to be something you read each day going through this challenge. Don't rush ahead, just read one day at a time and then do the daily challenge at the end of the devotion. Allow your imagination to run free as you go through a fictional journey in the six-week SOULCON Training Center with a group of eleven other men. Allow your mind and heart to be open to God's voice and be diligent to stay focused and finish each day strong. Remember, everyone will not be at the same place physically and that's okay. This challenge is more mental and emotional than physical. So even if you have physical limitations inhibiting you from completing a challenge, just focus on the next challenge. Focus on the camaraderie with your team and the work the Spirit is going to do in your soul. I pray you have a life-changing next six-weeks! **Leave it all on the field!**

THE SOULCON CHALLENGE OBJECTIVES:

- Pray the Lord's Prayer out loud, on your knees – EVERY DAY
- No carbs after 3pm from grains and breads (sweet potatoes, vegetables, and berries are the only carbs you can have).
  - Track your caloric intake in the book or on an app, just record everything except for your three feast days.
- Drink at least 64oz of water a day
- Exercise at least 30 minutes 5 days a week
  - Run, walk or crawl, two 5ks (3.1 miles) a week
- Before you leave home for the day do 40 push-ups (or as many as you can)
- Sleep 6-8 hours a night (excluding feast days)
- Evangelism: Hand out a total of ten Gospel tracts to people you don't know.

THE SOULCON CHALLENGE
DAY 01
THE ARRIVAL

If you love deeply, you're going to get hurt badly. But it's still worth it...

C.S. Lewis

After a long day of travel, two delayed flights, and a ride in a shuttle for over an hour; we finally made it to the SOULCON Training Center. As we looked around, we soaked in the beauty of campus. I can't remember the last time I smelled fresh pine, heard the sound of a calm wind blowing through the trees, or heard a river rushing, and we're only an hour away from a major city.

"This is it Tyler, we've arrived! You hear that brother? No babies crying, no cars honking, nothing but peaceful bliss."

"Yeah, I could get used to this," Tyler says.

Tyler has been my best friend for years. We have been through, what seems like everything together. From getting married to our wives, to having babies, Tyler is a guy that has been there for me constantly. We have experienced so much of life together. He is a friend I thank God for constantly. I refer to him as Jonathan, to symbolize the David and Jonathan relationship from the Old Testament. I give him a hard time that I am more like King David anyway, the warrior and the one the women sing songs about. Tyler and I have an incredible friendship, one where we can be men and not have to explain why we act the way we do. We joke, compete against each other, encourage each other to grow and develop in Christ daily and we have a blast. We both love our wives and children, but we cherish the times when we get to have time with just the guys. There is such a feeling of strength when we're together and I am excited about this journey we are about to embark on.

For the next six weeks we are going to live and breath this elite discipleship training called SOULCON we have read about. We have heard from men who have been through it, and we have been planning on attending for over a year. We both have butterflies in our stomachs for what's ahead of us and anticipation to meet the ten other guys that will be on our SOULCON team. Ten guys, like us, who counted the cost to be here. Who place the priority of growing in our knowledge of who we are in Christ and living in His strength above anything else.

We know our team will have twelve guys total. All whom have put their careers on hold and whom have most likely, like Tyler and I, been supported by their local church to be able to be here. Both Tyler and I were able to take the time off work, and we are so thankful our church has committed to helping support our family financially and emotionally while we're gone. One interesting aspect of this training center is the limited time to talk with your family. I've heard it's actually a prize for some of the challenges but not something that will happen regularly. Their focus here is to train men to get close to God, learn how to live with their soul in control of the Holy Spirit, and then go back home ready to lead their families and careers more effectively. Tyler and I both agree this is a great plan but we know it's going to be a challenge. We love our families like crazy, we love interacting with them, and we love doing life with them daily. But, we both know unless we are being led by the Holy Spirit we will be ineffective at leading our family and careers, and that's why we're here.

As we begin walking to the front desk to check-in we both continue to look around at the campus, our home for the next six weeks.

Tyler leans over and says, "This is where we are going to learn the art of dying to ourselves and living in Christ huh? At least the beauty of the campus can help distract us from the pain of discipline we are about to experience." Tyler has always been extremely optimistic and he is mentally stronger than most men I have ever met. I am thankful we are about to embark on this together. Mental toughness isn't a strength I have ever been able to boast in, but being married and having kids has certainly taught me a thing or two about it. Squats, running, push-ups, sit-ups and some of these extreme adventures might be another story. I trust Tyler will help me focus on the beauty around us rather than the painful work Christ will do in us. I know discipline is never easy… In our men's group back home we call it the "D" word, referring to it as a cuss word.

When we get to the counter to check-in, the guy there is extremely helpful, kind, and looks extremely fit. As we fill out the paperwork for our rooms, I ask the guy if he has been through this training.

"Yes sir, I have. I am so excited for the journey you're about to embark. Constantly remind yourself that it's about the mental and emotional strength in the Lord. The physical challenges are just a part of this challenge, not the main focus. So don't let those intimidate you. You'll make it if you decide that quitting isn't an option."

"Thank you sir," I said back to him. His answer was encouraging as well as challenging. Anxiety raced through my heart…. this guy looks like a true special forces soldier. If he was tempted to quit, Tyler and I might not stand a chance.

Tyler looks up, hands me my key, and says, "We've got this! You better worry more about getting shaving cream smashed in your face than us quitting. We have survived poopy diapers, wives with PMS and house work, this will be a cake walk."

"Good stuff! That's so true!" I said to him as I laughed. We finished our paperwork and headed to our rooms to unpack and get ready for our first team meeting.

After unpacking in our new homes for six weeks, which thankfully are right next door to each other, we both met back outside and headed off to our first class.

As we walked in I looked around at the other ten guys. I introduced myself to a few guys and took my seat. It was clear that everyone was a little nervous and out of their comfort zone. This helped calm my nerves a little. This course has a reputation of teaching men the art of dying to their sinful ways to truly live in Christ, to understand the importance of self-sacrifice, and not living for comfort. The words of the Apostle Paul in Philippians 1:21 are written on the board, and that happens to be one of my favorite verses.
"For to me, living means living for Christ and dying is even better." (NLT)

Even though this is one of my favorites, I am having such a hard time finding peace with this verse because of the nerves I'm feeling from the unknowns with this program. Everyone I talked to said this challenge will push me to my limit...and then a little further. Guys who have gone before me came to fully experience Philippians 1:21 when they went through this six weeks.

Anxious thoughts and emotions are flooding my mind and I begin to second-guess my decision to be here. The thought that I won't see my family until graduation day starts to weigh on my heart. Negative thoughts that I'm not cut out for this stuff, I'm too weak as a man, and I will never make it through this SOULCON challenge. With all these thoughts and emotions racing through my mind, our instructor walks in.

Yikes. This guy looks like an animal. This is not helping at all. He looks like he has never missed a day of working out in his life. What have I gotten myself into...

"Good Morning Gentlemen! My name is Commander Bugsly, and I count it an honor to be your instructor during your stay at SOULCON. We have quite a journey ahead of us. I am excited to guide you through this and see how the Spirit works in all of our lives over the next six weeks.

I hope you found your rooms okay. If you didn't let me know and we will get you taken care of. I want to make sure there are no logistical obstacles with housing during your stay here at SOULCON. You have more important challenges to focus your energy on."

Challenges? I hope this guy is talking about challenges for guys like me, and not for a guy like him! As Bugsly continues to go through the basic need to know items for our stay at SOULCON, my mind starts to wander and I begin surveying the guys in the room. This group of guys, our SOULCON team, is a diverse group of people. Some look extremely fit and others look as if they haven't run a day in their lives. My nerves begin to calm, knowing that all of these guys will go through this with me. The words of the guy that checked us in echo into my heart, "It's about the mental and emotional strength in the Lord. The physical challenges are just a part of this challenge, not the main focus. So don't let those intimidate you. You'll make it if you decide that quitting isn't an option." This time those words bring peace to my heart. I quietly thank God for a friend like Tyler who doesn't let me quit. He has been there with me through some of the darkest hours and he has constantly pushed me on. I believe we can do this... now I better tune back into this guy that looks like an MMA fighter and sounds like Liam Neeson.

"Alright, gentlemen. Let's dive into the most important topic of our stay here. In our world we have a plague negatively impacting the advancement of the Good News of Jesus Christ, the plague is the 'American Christian.' The person who thinks they are a Christian because of their church attendance, or because their family went to church growing up, or because they use Christian words when talking to the right people. Our main goal here at SOULCON is to train up warriors of God to share the Good News of Jesus to set people free from 'American Christianity' and experience true intimacy with Christ moment by moment. We want to make disciples who follow Christ with every area of their lives, not just in church on Sunday mornings. And this starts every morning by picking up our cross and denying our appetites to eat from the fork that feeds our flesh."

Sitting here listening to Bugsly explain the differences between a follower of Jesus and the "American Christian" I can't help but think of everyone I've come in contact with over the recent years, people who said they were Christians, but didn't follow Jesus with their actions. People who were more concerned with how they look in the mirror than what the Bible says about their life. People who enjoy sleeping in on Sundays more than waking up for church, or people who would take an invitation for a tee time over a church service. These people continue to run through my head...

Commander Bugsly continues on this topic with the message of the reality of hell, "The reality is, without soldiers of Jesus like you, people yearning to live fully committed to the calling the Commander in Chief has given you, these people who think they're Christians because of their label might not realize their need for Jesus as their personal Savior. These 'American Christians' might spend an eternity in hell if someone doesn't share the true Gospel with them. The time for men to live in the power of the Holy Spirit is now. This world needs more of Jesus and less of us, and that's the only way we will make a lasting impact during our short stay on this earth."

Commander Bugsly then begins to share stories from some of the greatest heroes in our faith, and the nervousness about this program transfer from fear to motivation in my heart. Bugsly breaks out his Bible and reads from Hebrews 11. As he reads the stories energize my soul. The motivation to carry out challenge flows through my body. I feel like I could go out into war right now! I'm pumped!

As Bugsly gets to the last part of the chapter, the part you aren't familiar with, you hear,

"...But others were tortured, refusing to turn from God in order to be set free. They placed their hope in a better life after the resurrection. Some were jeered at, and their backs were cut open with whips. Others were chained in prisons. Some died by stoning, some were sawed in half, and others were killed with a sword. Some went about wearing skin of sheep and goats, destitute and oppressed and mistreated. They were too good for this world, wandering over deserts and mountains, hiding in caves and holes in the ground." (Hebrews 11:35b-38 NLT)

Commander Bugsly closes his Bible, looks at our team and asks, "Are you, like these men listed in Hebrews chapter 11 too good for this world? Have you become so passionate about your mission from Heaven that the desire for things in this world or fears in this world has lost their power in your life?

It's my goal by the end of your stay at SOULCON that this message will be deeply rooted in your soul. I pray you will look at everything the world offers or threatens and have the confidence the heroes of faith in Hebrews chapter 11 had, a confidence with Christ in you nothing this world has to offer can compare. I pray you will learn to fully believe that who you are in Christ is more valuable than anything this world can offer. I pray that you realize fulfilling your mission from God tastes sweeter than any bite from the fork that feeds your flesh."

With that, he releases our team for our first coffee break.

DAILY CHALLENGE

Are you living for this world or the eternal world with Christ? What are some areas you can change in your life today that will allow you to share Jesus with others more effectively? Don't finish today without focusing on those areas. Ask the Holy Spirit to show you areas of your life that need developed with this. Commit to never submit to the "American Christian" lifestyle Commander Bugsly talked about. One of pretense but lacking true godliness.

COFFEE BREAK & COMFORT ZONES

If you want a religion to make you feel really comfortable, I certainly don't recommend Christianity.

C.S. Lewis

As our team breaks for coffee, I find myself sitting in my chair pondering the message Commander Bugsly just shared. What a challenge. I feel another wave of anxiety race over my body as I think about the areas in my life the Holy Spirit is going to work on during this challenge. Even though there are many areas I am pursuing Jesus with my life, there are areas where I am selfishly keeping Him out of His Lordship of my life. It feels like the Lord is starting to walk through my inner life with a flashlight. I am not thrilled about what He is going to find when I open some of the doors locked by selfishness. I know I haven't been living like the heroes in Hebrews chapter 11, but I have a longing in my heart to have that kind of courage, passion and selfless devotion to Jesus Christ and His Word.

Still deep in thought, Tyler walks up to me and nods his head toward the door. I slowly stand up, still in awe and fear of what the Lord is going to do in my life during this time.

"Man, what a challenge huh?" Tyler says as he puts his arm around my shoulder.

"I hear ya brother," were about the only words I could get out back to Tyler. I feel such heaviness in my heart for what the Lord is preparing to do in me. If you have ever played football you might know the feeling. It feels like a Friday night, the lights are on, the stands are full, and you're about to walk on the field to face the best team in your league. You have an excitement in your heart about the game, but a knowing deep within you that you're going to take some hard hits, face the temptation to give up, and be pushed hard the entire game. But even though you have these feelings, when it's time you run onto the field, soaking in the cheer of the crowd ready for war. That's how I feel in my heart. And I'm ready for war.

As we walk up to the coffee pots, a sign above the coffee pots grabs both of our attention. It has the SOULCON logo with these letters in all caps under it:

BLACK COFFEE PUTS HAIR ON YOUR CHEST.
CREAM AND SUGAR PUT YOUR HEART TO AN EARLY REST.
NEVER LET YOUR TASTE BUDS STOP YOU FROM LIVING YOUR BEST.

A few guys around us have a good laugh after we read this sign. "This place is pretty serious." I said to the guys, "I'm thankful we're all in this together."

Even though it's later in the day, everyone grabs a cup of coffee. I think everyone was a little fatigued from traveling and a little unsure about what the rest of this day had for us.

One of the SOULCON graduates came walking past us. I gave him a head nod and asked, "Was it worth it?"

He responded with an answer that would forever change my life as a follower of Jesus. He said, "SOULCON teaches you the only life on earth worth living is found in Jesus. After you realize you're dead to this world and alive in Christ, nothing can affect you. Nothing can stop you from picking up your cross daily. Nothing can steal your joy for living as a sacrifice for others. So yes it was worth it, just don't let your emotions convince you to quit before you finish."

"Right on! Thank you brother!" I say back to him, completely inspired and ready for what the Lord has in store for my life.

Tyler looks at me and does what most guys do in a serious time, he cracks a joke.

"I've heard this so many times that drinking black coffee puts hair on your chest, but I feel like the hair on my chest is running out of my body so it doesn't have to come in contact with the horrific taste of black coffee. At least we can practice crucifying our flesh sip by sip with this coffee."

The few guys standing around all got a good laugh at Tyler's cheesy joke as we took a sip of coffee and headed down the hall toward the classroom. While we're walking, I feel the peace of God flood my heart as I think about learning to truly live in Him. I will give anything to learn how to do that, even drink this black turpentine.

As we approach the classroom I look over at the sign on the wall right outside the classroom with a quote by C.S. Lewis and a picture of Jesus, bloody and beaten, carrying His cross up to Golgatha to be crucified.

"If you want a religion to make you feel really comfortable, I certainly don't recommend Christianity."

Tyler looks over at me, holds up his coffee cup and says, "Cheers! Goodbye comfort, here's to experiencing true life."

Walking back into the classroom, the picture I just looked at is consuming my thoughts.

"It's amazing what Jesus went through for us, so we can truly live. We have to keep His strength in suffering in our minds brother. It will make this challenge possible, even this black coffee," I said to Tyler.

"No kidding. It's easy to forget what picking up the cross daily truly means. I am so thankful we have such an incredible Lord to follow."

We both get back to our seats, sit down just in time for Commander Bugsly to open up with the question he closed the first session with, "So, are you too good for this world?"

Everyone on the team looks around at each other, then back at Bugsly and nod to signal yes.

"Good," Commander Bugsly says, and he continues teaching on what it looks like to be a follower of Jesus. As he's teaching my mind starts thinking about how this guy truly is a sold-out follower of Jesus. Certain areas of my life where I have become an "American Christian" keep popping into my mind. It is amazing how I am a grown man, but I feel like a child in some of these areas Bugsly is teaching about. But I promised myself before I came out here, nothing would stop me from learning to live like Jesus on this earth, and I know in my heart this is a lifelong process.

I finally focus my mind back to Commander Bugsly's message, as he opens his Bible to first John chapter two and reads verses 15-16:

"Do not love this world nor the things it offers you, for when you love the world, you do not have the love of the Father in you. For the world offers only a craving for physical pleasure, a craving for everything we see, and pride in our achievements and possessions. These are not from the Father, but are from this world.

There is such a deception in our society today about the love this world offers gentlemen. We have to stay focused and not get tempted by what this world has to offer. In my time, I have seen many good men fall thinking what this world offers can satisfy their soul. These pitfalls can be anything from their love of golfing on the weekends to the hot secretary in their office. If anything takes the place of the love of the Father in our hearts it will never live up to its promise. Everything we do as a soldier of Jesus Christ flows from our knowledge of the Father's love for us. When we are learning and growing in His love, there is no temptation that will move us off the path He has for our lives. Never forget you have an enemy that hates you and wants you and your families destroyed. Satan will never experience the love of the Father and it is his mission to stop you from experiencing that love on this earth. He knows when you experience a love so amazing, you will have the strength to overcome any obstacle, to resist any temptation, and it will be impossible for you not to share the Father's love for people with whom you come in contact with. It is God's unconditional love for us that has to remain our focus every day. Without our focus on His love and the joy found in His love, our soul will search for love in other places, and you know as well as I do, Satan and his demons are masters at subtle temptations that cause catastrophic damage. So stay focused, encourage each other and allow God's love to be the power that gives you strength in every area of your life."

With that Commander Bugsly closes our first meeting and gives us the schedule for the next day. As I look at the schedule my stomach sinks when I see the first meeting time. I look away and look back at the paper to make sure the black coffee isn't playing tricks on my mind, but sure enough the first meeting time is 0430 on the grinder.

"Wow, I guess this is how you learn to love coffee with no cream and sugar, wake up so early the only thing you focus on is the caffeine," I said to Tyler.

Tyler laughed and said, "This means you will have to wake up at 0300 to fix your make-up princess."

"Well played … well played." Tyler never misses an opportunity to give me a hard time for taking a little longer than most to get ready for the day.

"See you dark and early gentlemen! Let your alarm clock be your reminder that successful living in Jesus is only found outside of your comfort-zone." Commander Bugsly looks almost giddy at the fact we have to wake up so early. This is going to be one heck of an experience…

DAILY CHALLENGE

During your exercise time today ask the Lord to teach you to see the joy in suffering, ask that He shows you how to keep your focus on the joy before you and not the pain you're experiencing.

So be truly glad. There is wonderful joy ahead, even though you have to endure many trials for a little while. These trials will show that your faith is genuine. It is being tested as fire tests and purifies gold—though your faith is far more precious than mere gold. So when your faith remains strong through many trials, it will bring you much praise and glory and honor on the day when Jesus Christ is revealed to the whole world.

1 Peter 1:6-7 NLT

After what felt like a few minutes of sleep, a rush of adrenaline pulses through my body. It sounds like a fire alarm going off. As I reach over to turn the light on, there's no light. My brain finally catches up to understand what's going on…SOULCON. It had slipped my mind where I was. I reach over and shut off the alarm clock which is making the horrifically loud noise. I look at the time and it says 0400. I haven't seen 0400 on purpose in years.

At that moment a wave of emotions flood my body trying to convince my mind to quit this training program. Thoughts race through my head doubting why I'm here, and all I can picture is Commander Bugsly standing in the front of our class yesterday. Either this guy is the real deal, or he's a joke. I mean who refers to himself as "Commander"? This training center might be too extreme for me. Just then I hear my coffee pot finishing brewing. Here at SOULCON they encourage everyone to set their coffee before they go to bed just to remove one of the excuses of continuing to lay in the comfort zone of the bed. As the coffee finished, I knew it was time to decide. If I was going to quit, now would be the time, but I couldn't imagine telling Tyler. I am sure he's over there with a smile on his face ready for this challenge. I can't let him down… Dang.

Just then, the thought comes into my head of the theme of SOULCON:

Called to Sacrifice. Not to Comfort.

With that thought, I roll out of bed to grab a cup of coffee. "I am committed, I will finish this no matter what my emotions tell me." Just as I speak these words, I feel peace flood my body. I walk over to the chair in my room, get on my knees, and pray the Lord's Prayer out loud for my family and our SOULCON team. Then I thank God for giving me a healthy body, and I sit up to sip my coffee and read His Word.

At 0425 I lace up my running shoes, my new running shoes. I haven't put on running shoes, for the purpose of exercise, for years. It feels good. I feel like I am lacing up my boots for battle. I like it.

As I step out of my room at 0427, Tyler is standing between our rooms, sipping his coffee, and looking out at the training center. "Good morning, brother."

"Yes it is. Let's savor this brother. Just to clarify I am talking about the experience and scenery…not this black coffee." We both get a good laugh and get ready to go for our first SOULCON team run. As we walk up to the grinder we see Commander Bugsly standing there with the ten other team members. Bugsly looks like he's had five cups of coffee, and he has a smile on his face that looks a little sadistic.

As everyone gathers around, Bugsly starts to explain the mental side of what's about to happen. He explains the purpose of running and it's importance in the life of a Christian. How running teaches us to control our minds and emotions when we want to quit. Bugsly makes the statement, "In my opinion, the clearest way to hear the difference between the voice of the flesh and the voice of the Spirit is to start running. The voice yelling at you to quit, that you might die, that your knee might blow out if you don't stop, is the flesh. The Spirit will stay quiet until it's time for you to be encouraged, to be ministered to. Never forget the Spirit loves discipline. He wants us to learn to love it too."

Powerful. As he continues to talk my mind is racing thinking about what he said. Thoughts come racing through my mind about how true that is, and how I've seen that so many times in my relationship with the Spirit. Not with the running part, but how the flesh will scream constantly, but the Holy Spirit will be quiet until the right time to speak. How the Spirit loves discipline, and how He wants us to learn to love it too. I know in my heart this is true, but my mind still wants to refer to discipline as the "D" word. I have built up a hatred for discipline in my thinking, I guess it's time to change my thinking to be more like the Spirit.

Bugsly pulls out his Bible and flashlight and starts to read:

"So be truly glad. There is wonderful joy ahead, even though you have to endure many trials for a little while. These trials will show that your faith is genuine. It is being tested as fire tests and purifies gold—though your faith is far more precious than mere gold. So when your faith remains strong through many trials, it will bring you much praise and glory and honor on the day when Jesus Christ is revealed to the whole world. (1 Peter 1:6-7 NLT)

Bugsly challenges us, with his Liam Neeson sounding voice, to "Focus on embracing the physical pain during this first team 5k. Focus your mind on the purpose of why you're running. Think about your family, your loved ones, and the people you haven't met that need to hear the Good News of Jesus Christ from your mouth. Remember gentlemen, you are the hands and feet of Jesus. So stay focused on putting in the work to have a healthy body, a strong mind and emotions, and then the pain of running won't force you to quit. When your WHY is stronger than the resistance to change, you will prevail. Let's get going!"

DAILY CHALLENGE

Take a few minutes today and look up two benefits of the human brain and running. If you focus on the benefits of running, that information will help you push through the hard times when you want to quit. Remember, the only thing stopping you from living in optimal health is your motivation to keep fighting, to keep sowing seeds daily for your health tomorrow. Make sure you keep focused on your output and not the comfort of your current situation. Commit today to not let the desire for comfort stop you from putting in the hard work to be as fit as possible for Jesus.

Therefore we also, since we are surrounded by so great a cloud of witnesses, let us lay aside every weight, and the sin which so easily ensnares us, and let us run with endurance the race that is set before us.

Hebrews 12:1 (NKJV)

As our team starts out on the run, I feel all of the kinks working themselves out in my knees and ankles. I hope nobody can hear all of these pops and cracks. I start to think how long it's been since I ran a 5k...or even ran at all. Wow, that's an embarrassing thought. It's been years.

This reason is one of the main reasons I signed up for this extreme discipleship-training course. I have known for a while that God desires for me to take better care of my body, I just needed something to get me started on that track, something to give me motivation that will promote a lasting change with my health. I think SOULCON is just the thing I needed...

As our team gets a little over a half-mile into the run, one of the guys, starts to walk. Suddenly a sense of pride comes into my heart that I wasn't the first one to stop running, and my mind starts judging this guy for walking. "Come on! This is our first run and you're walking already?! You're going to slow the whole team down. Why did you even sign up for this training?" As I'm having these thoughts, Bugsly slows the whole team down to walk with this guy. We all slow to a walking pace, and I am guessing everyone is frustrated, like me, with Bugsly for slowing everyone down for one overweight guy. A guy who's at least 100 pounds overweight, and with his running stride, I question if he has ever run in his life.

I lean over to Tyler "Why did he even sign up for this challenge?!" Tyler looks at me and says, "Probably the same reason we did." Ouch.

Just then this guy starts talking to the group. "Guys, I am so sorry

I slowed us down. Please forgive me. I promise I will give it my all, everyday here at SOULCON. I need this training more than you know. If we haven't met my name is Alfred and about six months ago my daughter died from a long fight with cancer. She was brave until the end...but I wasn't. While she was suffering, I became resentful to the Lord and I sought comfort in food. I actually used to workout regularly, eat healthy, and loved Jesus like crazy. But when my daughter was diagnosed with cancer everything changed in my family, and in my life. My daughter fought cancer like a champion for seven years. A majority of the time I would leave work, grab my family dinner from a fast food restaurant, and go spend time with her in the hospital. During that time I got extremely out of shape and overweight. Once my daughter went to be with the Lord, and beat cancer by dying with a smile on her face, I turned to food like I never have before. I even contemplated suicide. I knew something had to change… I had allowed resentment and hurt to fill my heart instead of my love for Jesus. I had quit on life. One day my wife heard about the SOULCON Training Center and encouraged me to go. I immediately knew it was something I had to do, I was desperate. I knew if I didn't do this, I was going to give into the depression attacking my life. So please have patience with me...forgive me for walking, but please don't let me quit. I need you guys more than you know. I have an eight-year-old son and a wife that needs me present. They need me to lead them the way Christ has called me to. I need this training more than you know…"

My heart sinks. How can I be at an elite discipleship training center, focused on becoming more like Jesus, and be acting so sinful to a brother in the Lord? God, please forgive me. I need this more than I know…

As we are all walking, I speak up, "Guys, I know we just met yesterday, but I want you to know I need you as much as Alfred does. I have to confess and repent. When Alfred stopped, I became frustrated and judgmental. And honestly I have been doing that a lot in my walk with the Lord. It makes me feel better about myself. It helps lessen the pain of the knowledge I have of not being fully submitted to Christ in my life. I need everyone to keep me accountable with my judgmental attitude toward others. I want to be like Jesus in every area of my life, and I know there is nothing comfortable about that. Please help me, like Alfred to not give up. Let's make an agreement this morning to not let anyone give up...no matter how tough it gets. Sound good?"

Everyone on the team chimes in with agreement and we all walk/jog the rest of the 5k together, talking and getting to know each other. We finish the 5k amazed to see strength coming from what was thought to be an act of weakness. None of us will ever view Alfred the same, or anyone else for that matter. I know the Lord did a great work in my heart this morning. I feel set free from the weight of the judgmental sin that was ensnaring me. I'm ready to allow the Spirit to fully control my mind, will and emotions, and I think many of the others are experiencing the same thing.

DAILY CHALLENGE

Is there someone in you're life that you are judging? I challenge you to pray and ask the Holy Spirit to show you who that person is, and ask the Spirit to help you strip off that weighty sin so you can run your race with endurance. If you're struggling with this, text, call or email one of the guys on your team to pray for you.

For God has not given us a spirit of fear and timidity, but of power, love, and self-discipline.

2 Timothy 1:7 (NLT)

After getting cleaned up from the first team 5k, I met Tyler outside of our room to head into the chow hall to grab breakfast before our morning lecture. As we're walking, we see Alfred in front of us, "Alfred! Wait up!" Tyler and I both jog to catch up with him.

"I just want you to know how impressed I was with your transparency this morning brother. Thank you. And thank you for having the courage to come here. You have already made an incredible impact on my life."

"Thank you brother. God is so good. It's amazing how God can use our weakness for His glory. I am so excited and thankful to be here with you guys."

I put my arm around him and Tyler, feeling such a love for both of them, and we all walk into the chow hall. After the early morning 5k we're all ready to eat.

As we get to the line I remember that nutrition is a part of this training. Dang. My hopes and dreams are shattered. I had visions of steaming hot biscuits, thick white gravy, with bacon and scrambled eggs. What's in front of us doesn't look appetizing at all, these "eggs" don't have a hint of yellow. But I have committed to this training to honor God and serve others more effectively so I don't complain. I fill my plate with these crazy white fluffy things they call egg whites, I grab some oatmeal with no sugar or butter, and then I grab a piece of fruit. I walk over to grab a cup of coffee and again, I'm reminded this place doesn't have cream and sugar. "Embrace the pain" I say as I pour my coffee. With a smile I walk over to the table where our team is, and sit down.

Shortly after I sit down, Bugsly walks in, looking as tough as always, and he says with a smirk on his face, "Looks like everyone is enjoying their breakfast. Those egg whites are fantastic right?"

Bugsly then walks over, grabs his food, coffee, and sits down with the team. It seems almost awkward as the team nonchalantly watches him eat and drink this black stuff they call coffee. It actually looks like he enjoys this stuff…

Just then I start thinking of how much I miss that latte I would get each morning on my way into work with that delicious muffin. With that thought, I dig into my "food."

After we all finish up, Bugsly asks "How many of you guys enjoyed the taste of this food?" Comically nobody raises their hand. "Good, you're learning one of the best lessons of this program."

"What lesson?" Alfred asks.

"The lesson of discipline. Discipline is doing what you know is right even when you don't feel like it. God has called men to live disciplined lives…and our eating is included in that. You're going to learn all about that during your stay at SOULCON. But please never forget, discipline is never easy, but it's always worth it."

With that, breakfast is over. We take our plates to be cleaned off, and we head over to the classroom.

DAILY CHALLENGE

Have you been relying on your own strength to discipline your body with health? Have you been expecting to find the magical place where discipline is a bad memory? Spend some time in prayer today asking the Lord to reveal His strength to you in the disciplines of doing the ordinary, everyday things well.

THE LECTURE THAT CHANGED EVERYTHING

For God loved the world so much that he gave his one and only Son, so that everyone who believes in him will not perish but have eternal life.

John 3:16 (NLT)

I walk into the classroom for our morning lecture, sipping my cup of black coffee, I feel a sense of excitement to hear what Bugsly has to teach us. I'm really looking forward to growing closer to God with these men, and I can already tell the Holy Spirit is starting to work in my heart in the area of what Godly discipline truly is.

As our team gets seated, Bugsly begins his lecture:

"Good morning! I hope everyone is off to a great start! I promise this challenge will be one of the most life changing experiences of your life...if you allow it to be. We are going to cover so much, and myself along with a few guest speakers will help you understand the how of living as an elite soldier of Jesus Christ on this earth. I'm not just saying this because I'm an instructor here, but the message of the training center is one that transformed my life as a Christian man. The moment I learned how to live with my soul in control by the Holy Spirit and not my flesh, it changed everything for me.

There are so many different areas of the soul we're going to cover along this journey, but before we do, I have to lead you through a lecture on discovering your why for disciplining your body every week with healthy living.

I am sure, like most groups that come through this program you're wondering why people refer to me as Commander. I want to help you understand the importance of that title, and help you get to know me a little more. You see, I spent 27 years of my life as an active duty special forces member in the United States military. Throughout that time I lived my life as a person who partied just as hard, if not harder than I worked. I didn't know Christ during that time, and I did just about everything you could do as a partying special forces member in the military.

Two years after I retired from a career in the military, my life fell apart. My son and daughter were riding in a car after a long night of partying, unfortunately they were following in my footsteps. My son was driving, and it seemed like he was driving himself and my daughter from one party to another party. During that drive he lost control of the car, and he and his younger sister, they were 22 and 19, went off the road and crashed into a tree. They both passed away before they made it to the hospital.

I will never forget where I was when I got the phone call from my wife...my life was forever changed. I had so many emotions and thoughts flood through my mind and heart. I had no idea, at that moment where my kids were. I knew I didn't raise them with faith in anyone in the afterlife, I always told them to not trust anyone except their own family, not even a god. But thoughts kept running through my head like, what if I was wrong, what if there is a Heaven and what if there is a Hell?! Those thoughts rang in my head for months after they passed away...eventually leading to my breaking point.

One night I was in my room, looking at a gun I had laid out in preparation to take my life. My agony was so strong, and the depression was so high I couldn't bear it any more. It was at that moment; with my hands shaking I hit my knees. I cried out to God. I asked Him if he was real to help me. I asked Him to help me not do what I was about to do. At that moment, for the first time in my life, I felt peace and love fill my heart. Tears came rushing down my face... For the first time, while kneeling in front of the gun I had planned to take my life with, I met Jesus as my personal Savior. I committed to follow Him. That day changed everything...."

DAILY CHALLENGE

As you go through your day today, spend time thinking about the day you first met Jesus. How sweet it was, how personal it was, and how it was all about His love for you and not about any good work you have done. Ask the Holy Spirit to help you relive some of those emotions today. What a wonderful day that was for all of us...

THE LECTURE THAT CHANGED EVERYTHING (CONT.)

This means that anyone who belongs to Christ has become a new person. The old life is gone; a new life has begun!

2 Corinthians 5:17 (NLT)

"That day, the day I met Jesus as my personal Savior changed everything in my life. I was a grown man that never felt unconditional love in my heart, and I knew beyond a shadow of a doubt Jesus Christ was real, and He had just come into my heart. I stood up, put my gun back in the case, and walked out to talk to my wife. I had to share everything with her…

Praise God my wife received the Good News of Jesus too, and we have lived to serve Him from that point until now. We have accepted our mission as a couple to live and love where Christ has called us and to make disciples to do the same. I am so grateful for what Christ has done in my life, but I will never forget the emotions I felt when the people I loved the most on this earth died without knowing about the love and hope of Jesus Christ. That pain is indescribable…

I have made a pact with myself that I will never let that happen again. Evangelism will not just be an event in my life, or a mission trip, but it will be, for the rest of my life, every part of my life. I have decided to be more committed to the great commission of Christ than I was to this country, and that is why I'm referred to as Commander at this training center. I want the constant reminder of the dedication I had as a special forces Commander for this great country. I am committed to serve Christ with more honor, courage and commitment than I did this country.

Now, I want to take a look back at what Christ didn't do in my life at the moment of my salvation. What He did for you and what He didn't do at the point of your salvation is what we will focus on during the rest of our time at the SOULCON Training Center. Every time you eat, drink, sleep and exercise I want you to think about what Jesus did for you when you were saved…and what He didn't do.

You see, when I met Jesus as my personal Savior I know I was made completely new. I was born again into a new life. But there was a side of me that Jesus didn't make new, and that was an intentional act by Jesus. When I met Jesus He didn't reach down from Heaven and give me a completely new brain. He didn't remove the terrible memories I have from war. He didn't remove some of the images from the hippocampus in my brain that I have from being sexually active with different women. He didn't give me a new personality, which is found in the prefrontal cortex and frontal lobe of the brain. He didn't give me a new physical heart, and He didn't give me a new body. Jesus gave me the gift of the Holy Spirit, and that birthed my spiritual man. With the gift of the Holy Spirit and my new spiritual life, He gave me purpose and a mission in His Kingdom. And those things were 180 degrees opposite than the world I knew for my whole life. I didn't realize then, but I just stepped into a war that would last the rest of my life. This verse came alive to me:

'I say then: Walk in the Spirit, and you shall not fulfill the lust of the flesh. For the flesh lusts against the Spirit, and the Spirit against the flesh; and these are contrary to one another, so that you do not do the things that you wish.' Galatians 5:16-17

There is now a war that goes on inside of me everyday whether to live in the identity of my new man clothed in the Spirit, or to live under the control of the sinful urges of my flesh, the urges that used to define me. You see, there is a big difference from your personality as a human, and your identity in Christ. And when you live to know that difference, you can understand your WHY for life, you can know your new identity in Jesus and you can transform your mind and emotions to live and look like Jesus. Jesus longs to see His children understand the importance of living and walking in His power and strength, and not their own. He longs to see us controlled by the desires of the Holy Spirit and not the desires of the addictions in our brains. He longs to see us offer our bodies to Him as a sacrifice...every part of us. And that class," continued Bugsly, "is the WHY for healthy living in the Body of Christ. Stewarding the brain, physical heart, and muscular skeletal system that Jesus bought with the price of His blood on the cross.

Let's take a quick break and join back in 10."

DAILY CHALLENGE

Text or email someone on your team about how you're doing in the war between the Spirit and your flesh. Share with at least one person on your team one area is that you can ask the Holy Spirit to help you surrender to His control. Remember God loves us like crazy, and He is waiting for us to ask Him for help. And we need transparent accountability with our brothers in Christ.

WEEK 01 RESULTS

Be sure to share your results and encourage others
going through the challenge on the SOULCON App.

WEEK 01 REFLECTIONS

Be sure to share your reflections and encourage others
going through the challenge on the SOULCON App.

THE SOULCON CHALLENGE OBJECTIVES:

- Pray the Lord's Prayer out loud, on your knees – EVERY DAY
- No carbs after 3pm from grains and breads (sweet potatoes, vegetables, and berries are the only carbs you can have).
  - Track your caloric intake in the book or on an app, just record everything except for your three feast days.
- Drink at least 64oz of water a day
- Exercise at least 30 minutes 5 days a week
  - Run, walk or crawl, two 5ks (3.1 miles) a week
- Before you leave home for the day do 40 push-ups (or as many as you can)
- Sleep 6-8 hours a night (excluding feast days)
- Evangelism: Hand out a total of ten Gospel tracts to people you don't know.

The Christian does not think God will love us because we are good, but that God will make us good because He loves us.
                                                              C.S. Lewis

Walking out of that lecture to grab some coffee and a piece of fruit, I feel like my whole life just changed in that classroom. Honestly, I don't even feel like talking to anyone. I just keep thinking how I could have lived so long as a believer in Christ and not have been a good steward with my brain, physical heart and my muscular skeletal system. I have never really thought through the flesh before, but when Bugsly took us through his own testimony it opened my eyes to when I was born again, my moment of salvation. I remember the moment when I gave my life to Christ, and when peace and love flooded my heart and I knew I was made completely new. But I have never taken the time to focus on what Christ didn't make new at that time of salvation.

Guilt enters my mind for the way I have treated my brain since that point with some of the images I've looked at, with how unhealthy my diet has been, and how my life has lacked the needed exercise. I think about my physical heart health, and how I haven't done cardiovascular training since...well...high school. And my cholesterol levels...yikes! Just as I start to think about the lack of care I have given to my muscular skeletal system Tyler walks over to me.

"Hey brother" Tyler says in his always chipper personality. "Don't look so down, remember the words of C.S. Lewis:

'The Christian does not think God will love us because we are good, but that God will make us good because He loves us.'

Just because this teaching is hard, don't allow the negative thoughts that come in stay. Trust that God will help us become good because of His love for us, and fill your brain with those thoughts. Send those negative thoughts back to hell where they came from."

Throughout my friendship with Tyler it seems like he constantly knows the right encouragement for me at the right time. I am so thankful to share life with a man that loves the Lord like Tyler.

"Thanks bro, there are just so many areas I haven't been living the life Jesus deserves. I mean, He gave everything for me, and at times I just give Him weak lip service and a fake smile. I will accept the challenge and lean into this challenge like a man. I will embrace the pain of suffering, I will endure as I realize the areas in which I have been living to please my desires for my comfort. I know at the end of the day, my deepest desire is to live the life God has called me to. I want to thank Him and live my life as a sacrifice of thanksgiving for what Jesus did on the cross for me. I choose to depend on Christ in every area of my life, not just when it's a church event. Here's to living all in for Jesus!"

As I finish sharing that with Tyler, Bugsly calls people back in the classroom for the second half of this lecture. Tyler holds up his cup of coffee for a cheers, and I meet him in the middle, head back into the classroom, ready to develop in Christ.

DAILY CHALLENGE

Pray for an opportunity today to tell someone about the day you were born again. Ask the Lord to open an opportunity for you to minister to someone going through a hard time and share how God made you completely new. Make sure you have a tract with you that they can read after you talk with them.

THE LECTURE THAT CHANGED EVERYTHING (CONT.)

If anyone desires to come after Me, let him deny himself, and take up his cross daily, and follow Me.

Luke 9:23 (NKJV)

Walking back in to grab my seat I feel more now than ever the desire to learn how to follow Christ, and serve Him as a special forces soldier in His army. I am learning how following Jesus truly demands my whole life, not just some parts of it. The cost of being a disciple of Jesus is high, and it's one where your control is surrendered. But after experiencing God's love there is nothing else I would desire to pursue, so I'm all in. And for the first time in my adult life, I actually mean that. God is so good. And then Commander Bugsly starts speaking.

"One of my dear friends in the military would always remind me that pain is a great reminder we are still alive. You see, as a man on this earth, you're a leader, and every leader is married to pain. Leaders either have pain from growth, pain from regret, or pain from failure. It's necessary that we embrace pain and we don't fight to live a life of comfort. Jesus never said life would be comfortable, and this training center is focused on inspiring men to be excited about living uncomfortably for Jesus by picking up their cross and putting down the fork that feeds our flesh. For the record, picking up your cross is always painful, it's always a challenge, it always calls you out of your comfort zone, but I promise you will never regret it. Each morning when you start your day on your knees praying, make the decision to follow Christ fully, pick up your cross instead of feeding the appetites of your flesh, and you will find the true life in each day.

There is a strong spiritual battle waging war for men in the Body of Christ to live in comfort, to live passively to the darkness growing around them, to be sissies with their faith. And the cross of Jesus is a picture of the antithesis of these things. The cross of Jesus is hands down the most offensive thing in this world, and at the same time it is the greatest symbol of hope. When you pick up your cross and follow Jesus you are guaranteed a life of sacrifice, a life focused on laying your lives down for others in service; it is what we are called to and there is no greater joy. When you view this calling as a special forces soldier you start to understand it more. When someone joins the military for this country, they choose a special forces life not for fame, let me tell you, it's not for money, and it's definitely not for a comfortable life. Those men choose special forces in the military because of their love and honor for this country. I pray this is the same reason we all choose to show God we're willing to pay it all for His army. To be used as special instruments not for any motive other than love and honor to our King.

Let me tell you, once we all make this commitment, we find the battle we long to fight as men, the battle to save others from suffering, to love on people in hard situations, to live as someone's hero. We all long for it gentlemen, when we live like Jesus on this earth we get to experience it. But it will cost us everything.

I view each day of following Jesus with the same intensity and more than when I became a member of the special forces group for the United States of America. I knew what I was getting into when I enlisted in the military to be a special forces soldier. I didn't make the decision to be comfortable. I made the decision to do this to live as a sacrifice for others, to be a hero to someone who may never have the opportunity to thank me. I committed my life to be used as a special tool to keep this country safe from the attacks of the enemy, and I committed my life to be used to advance the strength of this great country. And that is what Christ is asking all of you here to do. He is asking you to lay down your desire for comfort, and commit to live elite to serve the mission of His Kingdom with your life. He is asking you to live as though you have already died to this world… because it's then, and only then, you can truly live for others. I want you all to look at the SOULCON logo. There's a skull for the logo because we want you to be reminded every day that you are dead to this world and alive in Christ through what He did for us on the cross. It's only in the cross that we find true life and passion. So if we view our lives as dead men to the things of this world, the desires of the fork that feeds our flesh loses its power. We pray you guys learn to live this every day for the rest of your lives."

With that comment, Commander Bugsly closed up his notes, passed out our week's agenda and told us he looked forward to seeing us at the grinder in the morning. Looking over the agenda, I thought about what Bugsly just said and knew this lecture had just changed my life. I knew without a doubt in my heart that I was ready to live fully surrendered to Jesus with my entire life...even my diet and exercise.

DAILY CHALLENGE

Do you view your life this way? Do you view your life as one of a special forces soldier? Dead to what the world offers and the lusts in it? Challenge yourself today and ask the Lord to show you what areas of your life are inhibiting you from living elite for Him. What areas can you grow in, or strip off so you can be the most effective as possible during your assignment on this earth? Commit to live everyday dead to this world and alive in Christ.

DAY 10
PUSH IT TO THE MAX

So then, since Christ suffered physical pain, you must arm yourselves with the same attitude He had, and be ready to suffer, too. For if you have suffered physically for Christ, you have finished with sin. You won't spend the rest of your lives chasing your own desires, but you will be anxious to do the will of God. You have had enough in the past of the evil things that godless people enjoy—their immorality and lust, their feasting and drunkenness and wild parties, and their terrible worship of idols.

1 Peter 4:1-3 (NLT)

A full week has passed here at the SOULCON Training Center, and my body actually wakes me up a little before the alarm clock. Bugsly taught us how our circadian rhythms would start to adjust to the early mornings and our bodies would start to wake up with greater ease the more we woke up at the same time. And he was right. As I lay here in bed, I see 0357 and think how glorious it is to not get the crap scared out of me by this alarm clock that sounds like World War III is starting.

As I reach over to shut off the alarm clock before it goes off at 0400, I hear the coffee pot beeping to let me know it's finished brewing. What a glorious noise. Joy comes over my body and I praise God for the ability to have the coffee already made by the time I wake up.

I roll out of bed, grab a cup of coffee and get on my knees to pray the Lord's Prayer. With thankfulness heavy on my heart, I feel so grateful for the Lord leading me to go through this six-week training program. I know what I'm learning from Bugsly and my classmates, is developing me into the man I'm called to be. The man I've always known I wanted to be, but just didn't have the positive male peer pressure to encourage living that life.

As I pray, I try what Commander Bugsly does. He shared with us after his time of prayer in the morning, before he gets off his knees he visualizes the Holy Spirit putting the armor of God on him. He said it helps him understand every day that not only do we have a flesh that desires things of this world, but we have an enemy that hates us and wants us dead. So I do it. I picture each piece being placed on my body, like a soldier ready for battle, in my God's armor. My heart fills with joy as I think about living as a warrior for Jesus on this earth. I have longed for the battle my entire adult life, now I am learning to see how Jesus needs me to fight. And I'm all in.

As I finish praying, I throw on my workout gear, and head out of my room. I walk over to knock on Tyler's door to make sure he's up and rocking, and sure enough, just like usual he opens the door with a smile on his face and says, "Good morning brother! I'm ready to train, ready to continue on this elite discipleship journey with my body, soul and spirit. I am ready to push myself to my perceived limit...and then a little further!"

"Amen brother, me too! Let's break through some of our mental limitations today!"

We get a quick hug, not the girly kind, the low sideways high five with the one arm wrap around. Then we head toward the grinder. Alfred comes running up behind us and puts his arm around both of us. He says, "I want you both to know I was thanking God for you this morning. Today is a big day in my life. My son turns nine today!"

"God is so good! We love you bro, and please tell him happy birthday from us!"

"I will! Thank you! And even though I wish I was right there with him, I am so grateful to be learning and growing in Christ with you guys. I know not only am I becoming healthier physically, but I am growing in my knowledge of my intimacy of Christ...and that's developing my soul (mind, will and emotions) into the husband and father my wife and son need. Here's to finishing strong and never going back to comforting myself with anything other than the presence of the Holy Spirit!"

"Amen brother," I say to Alfred as we all step onto the grinder with the other nine guys on our team.

Bugsly begins to speak, "Good morning warriors! I hope you're doing great! You have all done an amazing job so far, but I want to warn you, we have stepped into our next week of training. It's max week. A week to push your body harder than you ever have before, a week to show you and teach you that developing is never comfortable. The theme of this week is learning you have no idea what your max truly is. Learning to break through your mental limitations to live beyond your comfort zones. I believe you can push yourselves ten times harder than you think you can. And I promise, like I was taught in my special forces training, you're only easy day in life was yesterday. So before we run this morning let's do three max sets of push-ups. Any break you get today, knock out a max set of push-ups, you're working on finishing the day with as many push-ups as possible. Day three of this week will be max sit-up day and day five will be max squat day. It's going to be a blast! Remember, the words in 1 Peter 4:1-3:

'So then, since Christ suffered physical pain, you must arm yourselves with the same attitude He had, and be ready to suffer, too. For if you have suffered physically for Christ, you have finished with sin. You won't spend the rest of your lives chasing your own desires, but you will be anxious to do the will of God. You have had enough in the past of the evil things that godless people enjoy—their immorality and lust, their feasting and drunkenness and wild parties, and their terrible worship of idols.' (NLT)

Let's practice living this out with our push-ups, sit-ups and squats this week. Let's practice the art of suffering well physically to bring glory and honor to God. Remember, everything we do here is to teach you how to walk in the Spirit and not the flesh with your mind will and emotions. We could care less about how ripped you are, how good you look in the mirror, or how many abs you have showing at one time. Our focus is to teach you the joy of making your body a servant to the mission God has called you to, and our hope is you never become a servant to the desires of your body."

DAILY CHALLENGE

As you push yourself with your max reps this week, don't just view it as a physical challenge. You will miss it completely. Pray the Holy

Spirit shows you how to learn from the pain you feel from your max days, and ask the Spirit to show you how to identify the voice of the flesh screaming to quit and His voice. Challenge yourself to push past your mental and emotional limits today and this week.

DAY 11
PUSH IT TO THE MAX

*The good Lord gave you a body that can stand most anything.
It's your mind you have to convince.*

Vince Lombardi

I did it. I did over 750 push-ups in one day…752 to be exact. I never, ever would have imagined I could do that many push-ups in one day. I had no idea what my body was capable of, and it was amazing how mental and emotional it was. There were so many times my flesh would tell me to quit, that I couldn't possibly do another push-up, and then I would do ten more. Praise God! I am learning to live this SOULCON lifestyle. I actually enjoyed pushing my body harder than I ever had in my life with push-ups. Knowing the guys on our team were doing it with me, pushed me when I wanted to quit. It reminds me of what Bugsly says, "Motivation inspires you to start, accountability inspires you to finish, strong."

There was a point yesterday when I had completed 250 push-ups, and my mind was telling me I was done, that there was no possible way I could do more. Then I talked to Alfred and he let me know he was at 300 and feeling strong when it was only 1330. He encouraged me to keep pushing, and I did.

I honestly was amazed that I finished the day with 752 push-ups in the bag. I hope this thankfulness continues as I try to use my arms today. I am worried that I might not be able to shampoo my hair or hold my coffee cup, but there is actually a side of me that's starting to enjoy the soreness…

After a great start to the day, and the surprising success with shampooing my hair, I walk into the classroom for today's lecture and notice everything looks different. Commander Bugsly is dressed like a monk and there are no chairs in the class, just large bean bags. The classroom smells like a candle store with the incense burning at different places in the room.

Bugsly welcomes me in and asks that I find a seat. I look over at

Tyler and Alfred, and give them a smirk, knowing Bugsly has an interesting lesson in store for us. But I'm ready. I'm slowly learning to trust this guy.

Bugsly starts to teach, "Good morning gentlemen. I want to congratulate you on making it through your first max day! I hope you took some time this morning to celebrate your victory with the Lord. Every time we find success or experience hard learning lessons we should spend time praising Him for leading and guiding us. What a wonderful God we serve.

As you walked in you probably wondered why I am dressed like a monk and I am excited to tell you. One thing I learned when I was 16 years old was the power of my mind. And to most people's surprise I did not learn this from a Christian. I learned it by spending six-months in a Buddhist monastery. My father sent me there to teach me how important focusing my mind was, and that time has forever impacted the reminder of my time on this earth. And today, I want to teach you what I learned from people who don't have the power of the Holy Spirit, but have more trained minds than most Christ followers.

There were two things we did during the course of that six-months, and I promise if you apply these things, you will forever be changed. I pray you accept the challenge from me to not let a Buddhist be more disciplined for their faith than you are for your faith in the King of kings and Lord of lords.

The first thing the Buddhists taught me during my stay there was that suffering has a cause. They taught me that we suffer because we are constantly struggling to survive. I was constantly reminded there that the harder we struggle to establish our relationships and ourselves the more painful our experience becomes. But it will always be worth it. They practiced this everyday in their lives in that monastery by not eating after 1530. They viewed the afternoon and evening as great times to experience hunger pangs, identify them, and overcome them. They taught me those pangs would come in waves and by overcoming them it would help me overcome the pressures in my life like wanting to quit, to lose control, to overeat, or to do anything else to harm myself or the world around me. They taught me that overcoming those hunger pangs would be the constant practice I need in the offseason to be prepared for true suffering when it was game time. What a valuable lesson…

And one of the many things I love about your stay here at SOULCON is having each student eliminate carbs in their diet after 1500 every day except for their feast days…that will start after Hell Week. You will feel the pangs of your body wanting carbs at night, but you overcome those urges and feed your body what it needs. View these times as practice. Practice for when the real temptation is on. If you practice submitting your mind, will and emotions (soul) to the Spirit with your hunger after 1500, it will be easier when stronger temptations come at you. You will be ready."

DAILY CHALLENGE

Pray for the Holy Spirit to teach you today and throughout this challenge for you to see the lessons to be learned with your strict diet and exercise program. When you feel hunger pangs today take time to pray and ask the Spirit for strength to let those feelings pass. View these opportunities like practicing free throws and lay-ups. These fundamentals might not seem important when the gym is empty, but it seems every great game comes down to the simple shots, the fundamentals players were practicing with nobody watching. Let's commit to be excellent in every area of life for Jesus. He is worthy.

And now, dear brothers and sisters, one final thing. Fix your thoughts on what is true, and honorable, and right, and pure, and lovely, and admirable. Think about things that are excellent and worthy of praise.

Philippians 4:8 (NLT)

"The second thing I was taught at the monastery was the art of meditation. I believe this is an art lost in the Western Civilization Christian Church and it is our goal at the SOULCON Training Center to bring a revival to the Body of Christ in this area. When I was in the monastery we would spend hours every day being aware of the feelings and thoughts of our bodies. We would use our imaginations to focus on not allowing the external activities around us to distract us from the peace and joy on the inside of us. They constantly taught these words from Buddha:

'We are shaped by our thoughts; we become what we think. When the mind is pure, joy follows like a shadow that never leaves.'

So we practiced developing in this. And it was fascinating to see these kind men I was with always content but never satisfied. They were always hungry for more peace, joy and purity and kept developing to obtain those traits. They desired enlightenment more than satisfying their current desires for pleasure in that moment. It was truly amazing for me to experience at such a young age.

It was so incredible learning this from these men, but it breaks my heart thinking about how these men had such a commitment to an empty religion. A religion with a destination of an eternity without Jesus, and eternity suffering the worst suffering anyone can imagine. Men, we have to have a passion in us to go into this world to preach the Good News of Jesus and a passion so strong to make disciples it bubbles out of us in every area of our lives. There are so many good people out there that will burn in Hell for eternity if we aren't diligent about sharing who Jesus is and what He did for everyone. The Good News is a message we are commanded to take into the world, and it is our joy to do this. It is our responsibility to share the Gospel, but it's God's responsibility to save people. We will discuss this more later, but we follow the orders given to us. We have to boldly preach the Gospel. We have to live fearlessly. If we truly love like Jesus, we shouldn't be okay with people living around us not hearing about the cross of Jesus from our lips and actions. That's why we're all here, to learn the importance of being so full of Jesus that we desire nothing else. So full of Jesus that we can't help but tell others, and meditation is one of the most effective ways to make sure our souls are full of Jesus.

For the rest of this day, we are going to practice the art of meditation for three hours as a class. This training will help you when you go back home and only have two to three minutes before you go to bed. This training today will teach you how to use those two to three minutes and calm your brain, focus on God's goodness, and then hit your pillow to sleep better than you have in years.

After learning and practicing mediation you will grow hungry for these times, times of being still in God's presence, thinking about His goodness, love and peace. You will be constantly aware of the positive impact mediation will have on your brain, your physical heart, and your muscular skeletal system. I pray you never forget the importance of allowing the Spirit to calm you internally no matter what external pressure is being applied."

DAILY CHALLENGE

Take five minutes today and focus on one word. That word could be peace, joy, love, hope or anything you choose. Pick that one word and use your imagination to think about things in Heaven. Think about detailed images, feelings and even textures of some of the plants, ground and water in Heaven. Learn to use your imagination to change your body when your external surroundings stay the same.

As iron sharpens iron, so a friend sharpens a friend.
Proverbs 27:17

As our SOULCON team walks into the chow hall, after three hours of mediation, I'm really excited to talk to them about what we just experienced. I mean, we just spent the last three hours meditating. That's pretty crazy. I didn't believe I could spend five minutes in meditation, let alone three hours. I can't even remember the last time I had thirty minutes of quiet in my life. Even in my devotion time, it's me reading, or praying, not being quiet and still before the Lord. I feel like a new, refreshed man.

Walking through the food line, I have a different perspective as I look at the lean meat and veggies. What Bugsly said about his time in the monastery, how the Buddhist Monks view hunger pangs as a way to develop in self-mastery inspires me to quit whining about the healthy dishes here. To look at them as practice, as a workout for my emotions to embrace the pangs of discipline knowing there is a future reward. So I put the correct portions on my plate, and I walk over and sit down. Our team prays together, giving thanks to God for the food, and the incredible experience He has blessed us with to this point. As we finish our prayer, we all begin eating. I tell the group how thankful I am for their friendship, and how much it means to me that we're all in this together.

One of the guys on the team, a guy who is thin and has more degrees than anyone I've ever met, Gage, chimes in.

"I have to tell you guys, this is one of the most incredible experiences I have ever had. As most of you know I have been in the church my whole life. I don't have a dynamic background and honestly, I have been sheltered in my life. I praise God for parents that loved me and always had me in church, but I have never lived to push myself, I have always lived to be comfortable in my 'Christian bubble.' I have always known I have had a warrior inside of me, but I didn't know how to let him out. Going through this training with you all helps me understand the fearless life God desires for us men to live. I have been praising Him since Commander Bugsly's first lecture, I finally see serving Christ as the adventure that it is. I am tired of living to be comfortable, I confess to you, my brothers in Christ that I will live the rest of my life as an honorable sacrifice of service and not a life focused on comfort."

Then Tyler slowly stands up. I know what's coming because Tyler is, and always has been one of the most motivational men I have ever known. Tyler holds up his glass of ice water for a cheers.

"I am with Gage! I commit to making SOULCON a lifestyle.

What Bugsly taught us today, with how to use our imagination to change the physiological state of our bodies is something I have never learned. When he had us shut our eyes and imagine the scary movies, then the hammock on the beach, then the horrible traffic jam, I actually felt like I was right there in each setting. I had no idea the impact the deep thoughts in my life had on my body. From here on I will be aware of it, and I will practice meditating each night before I go to bed. Please hold me accountable with this, I want to make meditation as much a habit in my life as brushing my teeth before I go to bed. Please know I love and appreciate you guys! Here's to never looking back, here's to finding contentment in suffering and happiness, and here's to learning we are 10 times stronger than we think we are. Here's to never, ever giving up!"

Just as Tyler finished, we stood and cheered. Right here, is right where God wants me, and the joy is indescribable. There's a sense of honor and excitement as I stand in the presence of warriors. Men of God who are committed to living all for Jesus, who are willing to go into hell on this earth to spread the Good News.

I am excited to push myself tomorrow with these guys with max sit-up day and then again with the max squat day later this week. I know these challenges will help all of us continue to develop our minds, wills, and emotions to be the men God desires for us to be. God is so good...

DAILY CHALLENGE

Take seven minutes today and practice meditation. Use the word you picked from yesterday, and focus on that word for seven minutes without interruption. The word I use is peace and I visualize myself sitting on a boulder with Jesus, in Heaven, looking at a waterfall with a Hawaiian style forest. It helps me feel peace and it opens my heart to hear the voice of our Lord.

No discipline is enjoyable while it is happening—it's painful! But afterward there will be a peaceful harvest of right living for those who are trained in this way.

Hebrews 12:11

Rolling over to shut the alarm off, it's the morning of the first day of the third week. My whole body feels the soreness from Max Week. As I lay there I start praising God for the journey He has led me to take at the SOULCON Training Center. I know I will go back to my family transformed by the Spirit.

I am so excited to love and lead my family in the Spirit, living in SOULCON. I know there are so many times I have overlooked the importance of living a disciplined life... and I know that has impacted my family negatively. There are so many areas I can change when I get home, everything from the food in our refrigerator, to the information I fill my brain with on the television. It's going to be incredible to live a focused, elite life for Christ when I return home, but I have a long way to go before this training is finished.

Someone knocks on the door, and I look at the clock knowing we're not supposed to be anywhere for 30 minutes. I walk over to the door and open it, Tyler is putting his shoes on as he tells me to grab my stuff. The Founder of SOULCON is calling for an early meeting on the grinder. So I grab my stuff, a little frustrated at the surprise meeting and at the same time, a little excited to meet the Founder of this training center.

As we jog to the grinder, we see the rest of the team heading that way as well. When we get to the grinder we see Commander Bugsly and the Founder of SOULCON standing with a table on either side of them. On one table there are hot, delicious looking donuts with lattes, and on the other table are the SOULCON Dog Tags. This is going to be interesting...

Commander Bugsly opens up, "Good morning! I hope you all got enough beauty sleep! As you can tell today is starting off a little different. Today marks your first day of week three. Congratulations for making it this far! We now enter into our two most difficult weeks of this training course, Fast Week and Hell Week. These two weeks are going to be the most crucial learning weeks of this program and I'm excited to see the transformation that's going to take place in your lives. I know when I went through this program these two weeks changed my life as a follower of Jesus. It was in these two weeks I learned the true importance of leaning on the Holy Spirit for comfort and strength and not using the fork that feeds my flesh. And when I went through this course my instructor was the Founder of this great institute, and I am so honored he's here with us today. He is going to spend all day with us as we learn the importance of our daily choices with our call to live a life of fasting. So without further ado, here is the man who God has used to start SOULCON."

"Good morning! I am so honored to be here with you all. Thank you for taking the time out of your lives to come and go through this program. As you know, this six-week journey is full of early mornings, unique physical challenges, life changing information, great teaching, and most importantly, teaching men to live in SOULCON. Every person on staff or who attends the course understands the importance of living with our soul in control by the Spirit and not by our flesh. We all focus our energy to live a SOULCON lifestyle and I pray by the end of this you will too. I look forward to instructing your class today along with Commander Bugsly but first I want to give everyone of you a choice.

As you can see there are two tables in front of me. One table represents the tables of the churches in America, the lattes and delicious donuts; on the other table there are SOULCON Team Dog Tags. I want you to choose this morning, and I pray it's something you never forget. If you choose the donut table, I will make sure SOULCON reimburses your money for the training and books a flight home for you tomorrow. If you choose the dog tag, you commit to be a change agent in your home church. You commit to make disciples with the importance of healthy living with the purpose of loving God and serving others. You commit to take a stand against the acceptable sin of being controlled by junk food, or any other lust of the flesh in the Body of Christ. If you take a dog tag you commit to be a part of the SOULCON movement in this world. One, I pray, that reverses the epidemic of men ideally sitting by in this world by one man at a time committing to live as a special forces soldier for Jesus. I have been called to inspire people to realize the dangers of feeding their flesh, and passive living is one of those areas for men in the Church today. It comes down to a decision for each of us. Giving our lives to serve and love others for Jesus, or giving into the desire to comfort and nourish our flesh. This morning is your moment to choose. On the other side of the dog tag is your first run over a 5k. We are heading out on a 6.2 mile team run this morning. Our goal will be thinking the whole way of the importance of men taking a stand with our health in the Body of Christ. So choose now, and for everyone who picks a dog tag we will take off in two minutes."

For me this choice is a no brainer. Even though I would love to go see my family and have money back in my pocket, I know this training is worth its weight in gold. Tyler and I look at each other and nod, and then we walk up and grab our dog tags with pride and walk to where the run will start. And to our surprise, nobody went for the donuts and lattes. Our SOULCON team has officially been established. Praise God. Now, time to start the longest run to this point of my life…

DAILY CHALLENGE

Think about how to encourage your local church to offer healthy snacks on Sunday if they don't already. Don't be the annoying person that just complains about a problem, but think of a solution. The truth is healthy food costs more than junk food. So maybe an option would be start a fund allowing people to give to healthy options on Sunday mornings. As a man we are called to humble, servant leadership, so don't approach this issue or any issue of life with pride. But commit to help make a change in your church in this area. Remember as a man, people will follow your leadership decisions. Talk to at least one person via text, email or a call today about possible solutions in your home church. Not eating healthy is like any other area of feeding our flesh, we have to be aware of the dangers, and encourage others to live free from those destructive habits.

WEEK 02 RESULTS

Be sure to share your results and encourage others
going through the challenge on the SOULCON App.

WEEK 02 REFLECTIONS

Be sure to share your reflections and encourage others
going through the challenge on the SOULCON App.

THE SOULCON CHALLENGE OBJECTIVES:

- Pray the Lord's Prayer out loud, on your knees – EVERY DAY
- No carbs after 3pm from grains and breads (sweet potatoes, vegetables, and berries are the only carbs you can have).
  - Track your caloric intake in the book or on an app, just record everything except for your three feast days.
- Drink at least 64oz of water a day
- Exercise at least 30 minutes 5 days a week
  - Run, walk or crawl, two 5ks (3.1 miles) a week
- Before you leave home for the day do 40 push-ups (or as many as you can)
- Sleep 6-8 hours a night (excluding feast days)
- Evangelism: Hand out a total of ten Gospel tracts to people you don't know.

So let's not get tired of doing what is good. At just the right time we will reap a harvest of blessing if we don't give up.
Galatians 6:9 (NLT)

As our team sets out on our first run over 3.1 miles, I'm feeling more honored than ever before to be on this team…I'm ready for war. It is finally sinking in that being a soldier in the Body of Christ is a daily war. It is a thrill ride with incredible highs and extremely painful, refining lows. And I understand more than ever the importance of healthy eating and exercise along this journey of being a good soldier of Jesus Christ. A sense of healthy pride wells up in my heart…honored to serve Christ fully.

After about three miles the Founder of SOULCON asks everyone to take a break and grab a sip of water. Our team has never run on this trail before and I am sure everyone, like me, is a little curious about where we're going.

The Founder then begins, "I want you all to know where you are standing is one of the most important locations of my career. It was right here, watching the sun come up, that I almost quit on my vision to see this training institute be born. I had been through so many things at that point, and everything in my life told me to quit. Even my wife, who is an incredible woman of God was growing weary. I was feeling pressure from every angle to let this dream go. But I knew the Lord was working in my heart to not give up, to press on just a little bit further. I cried out to God on my knees and asked Him for strength and endurance to continue to run the race He had set out for me. At that moment I felt the peace of the Holy Spirit flood my heart. God is so faithful.

But I wanted to point out something from that story on our run together this morning, and it's something I think about every time I run. This quote from one of my favorite motivational speakers of all time summarizes it the best:

'Mental toughness is many things and rather difficult to explain. Its qualities are sacrifice and self-denial. Also, most importantly, it is combined with a perfectly disciplined will that refuses to give in. It's a state of mind — you could call it character in action.' -Vince Lombardi

What I realized at that point in my life is there are no shortcuts to mental toughness. If you want to be mentally tough, you have to develop it. You have to learn to persevere in hard times as a man of God, and you cannot learn perseverance in comfort. Mental toughness only comes through tough times…there are no shortcuts.

On that day, when I was in this spot, crying out to God, I felt peace flood my heart, but I still had to stay committed in my mind and emotions to not quit. And that was difficult…even with God's peace in my heart. At the time, I was working to fundraise the building for this institute and I had eight months to raise $2.87 million or everything would be taken away, including my most valuable asset, the time I was devoting to this project.

But I just knew God was leading me…I knew this training center would be to glorify Him. I knew there would be a war, but it was a war that almost broke me…it almost made me quit. But as long as I had God's peace, I knew I could endure the pain of waiting for the completion of this project. From that point forward I knew, I did not doubt it again in my heart, that I had God's peace to proceed, but I had to remind myself daily. It wasn't until almost eight months later a donor came to me letting me know he wanted to write a check for this project as well as give to the funding for the next three years of operation. Praise God! I actually ran back out to the exact location you're standing and spent time on my knees worshiping God for His faithfulness! Praising Him for teaching me to trust Him.

What I learned was, in my opinion, the most valuable lesson a soldier in God's army can learn is what it takes to not give up when you're tired and weary: to trust God, to stay on the course, and keep running your race. I remind myself of this every time I run. And honestly men, running is hard every time I do it. But I remind myself everything good in this life doesn't come easy. And I no longer desire anything easy in my life. I want to lean into the battle, I want to wage war on this earth for God's Kingdom, and the strength to mentally persevere in that war is practiced in my life every time I am running. Every time I run I remind myself, out loud with self-talk that I am not a quitter. I make an excuse to win in that moment because I know it's developing me to win when the real life pressures are on.

So let's keep running and finish our 10k and remember how important it is to overcome the desire to quit. Please never forget that the more you practice this in your physical conditioning, the more developed you become when the spiritual warfare starts to wage. Let's get going…"

DAILY CHALLENGE

During your workout today, practice out loud self-talk. Practice growing in the art of encouraging yourself to win. When your mind screams that you can't, that you need to quit, practice speaking God's word over your life, out loud. Practice this when it's just exercise, when the demonic temptations come in you will be trained and ready for battle.

DAY 16
THE DOG TAG

In reading the lives of great men, I found that the first victory they won was over themselves… self-discipline with all of them came first.

Harry S. Truman

Well, I did it. I ran 6.2 miles for the first time in my life and what I learned along the way transformed who I am. I will never again run without thinking about practicing perseverance when the going gets tough. What an incredible experience this has been to this point, and we still have so much time left. As I reflect on this experience, I can't help but fall to my knees and thank God for His goodness and mercy in my life to get me where I am.

"God thank You for not quitting on me when I was not using the discipline You have given me in the Spirit. Thank you for loving me even though there are areas where I have been destroying my brain, heart and muscular skeletal system. I know you bought all of that with the price of Jesus's Blood on the cross. I ask you from this day forward to help me love you with my heart, soul, mind and strength. I praise You for the unconditional love You show me constantly. Thank you Lord. You are so good."

After taking time to rejoice and thank God for His goodness I am eager to see what's on the SOULCON Team Dog Tag. I reach over and grab the dog tag that was on the table this morning. I study it for the first time. On the front is the SOULCON skull, signifying a soldier of Jesus being dead to the passions and lusts of this world and alive through the cross of Jesus. Behind the skull is a fork pointing down with a snake crawling up it and a cross on the other side pointing up. Matching the theme of the program of putting down the fork that feeds your flesh and picking up the cross DAILY. We have constantly been taught how the fork that feeds our flesh loses its power in our lives when we are dead to our earthly appetites, like special forces soldiers are who go into battle. This is a lifestyle that starts every morning by picking up our cross and committing to live in Christ, for Christ and not in control by the desires of our flesh.

The whole idea of living with other men as warriors for Jesus makes me so excited to go back and live as a disciple of Jesus in my city. To share this information with different groups of men and take them through this journey together. Taking what I have learned so far and training disciples could start a revolution in my city. I want to share the beauty of disciplining your body by yielding your mind, will and emotions to Jesus. Trusting He will bring you true and lasting delight instead of the momentary satisfaction of sin. I am so pumped!

I turn the dog tag over and see the main verse of SOULCON:

> If anyone desires to come after Me, let him deny himself, and take up his cross daily, and follow Me.
>
> Luke 9:23 (NKJV)

I love it! I absolutely cherish the decision I made to pick the dog tag over the donuts and latte. For the record, I love both donuts and lattes, so that was a big decision for me. For the first time in my Christian walk I feel overwhelmed with joy because the Spirit is teaching me the strength in self-sacrifice.

Not knowing what's in store for the day, I am ready for anything. I put my dog tag over my head, and wear it with pride. This dog tag is my choice to give my all for Jesus and service to others with more pride than anything else in my life, even the colors of my favorite sports team back home. To me this is a big day. I desire to be more consumed with Jesus than anything else in my life…even something near and dear to my heart like college football. Wow. God can truly make the impossible, possible. My wife is going to be impressed!

DAILY CHALLENGE

Take time today and ask the Spirit to help you fall more in love with Him than anything else in your life. Ask Him to set a fire in your soul, a fire that will burn up any love you have for idols in your life. This is a surgery the Spirit will do on all of us, and it hurts every time, but it's always worth it. Lean into the fire today trusting the refinement is worth the momentary pain.

If you're ready to make this commitment, order your dog tag here: soulcon.com.

Wear it with pride, and let it be your commitment to change the world around you for Christ as a good soldier of Jesus Christ.

A wise person thinks a lot about death, while a fool thinks only about having a good time.

Ecclesiastes 7:4 (NLT)

As I sit down for today's lecture, I focus my mind and heart to be challenged and transformed by the Spirit. Commander Bugsly and the Founder are at the front of the class and Bugsly begins to speak, "Good morning class! I want to personally congratulate all of you on making the choice to stay at this training center as well as completing the longest run so far. What you are doing at this center will have an impact on the rest of your lives...I promise. And today is something that changed my life when I first went through this program. I will never forget the time I wrote my Letter. I had never put my life in perspective like that before...and I have done some crazy things.

I remember on some of my special operations deployments I had teammates who would spend time writing to their loved ones, writing the letter their family would read if they were dead. I have vivid memories of the emotions some of them would experience during this time, and honestly I didn't have the courage to write that kind of letter. I never faced emotions at that point in my life, because before I knew Jesus I only knew how to handle emotions by acting in rage or ignoring them. So, I never sat down and wrote a letter, that letter to my family, and I knew it was a risk. I lost a lot of great friends in war, men I consider family to this day. I knew it could be my turn at any moment. But I thought death would be easier than facing the emotions of never seeing my family again.

So when I went through this training, I remember sitting in your chairs, having my world rocked with what following Christ with every part of me looked like. I remember the run where we decided between the sweet food and drink and the SOULCON Team Dog Tag. Just a symbol of committing to serving others or living for comforts, but it was a monumental day in my life. And then I remember walking into this class, with the Founder here delivering one of the most difficult challenges I have ever heard. The challenge was the same as our challenge today, it was to write The Letter. I knew what this challenge was as soon as I saw the title on the board. I knew the Holy Spirit was going to make me confront this emotion head on. And I did it...

So here I am, with the Founder, ready to give you in my opinion the most difficult challenges you will face. We are going to take the next hour and write a letter to our family. A letter that is only to be read after we are dead, and this letter is apologizing for not using the discipline the Holy Spirit has given us. This letter is letting your loved ones know they were not as important as your desire to overeat, to live a sedentary life, to work non-stop, to do whatever it was by which your flesh was controlling you. This letter is one of death by the fork that feeds your flesh...

So get to a place where you take this seriously, and actually write this to your family. Allow your emotions to come out. I personally believe it's this realization that stops me from ever allowing the desires of my flesh to overtake me. I pray this letter impacts you as much as it did me..."

DAILY CHALLENGE

Write this letter. Pretend you allowed the fork that feeds the flesh to overtake you. Use your imagination to visualize your weakest area consuming you. For me it would be not controlling my passion to work and allowing my exercise to slip. If I allowed that by feeding those desires, bite-by-bite my blood pressure would increase from too much stress and lack of exercise. My family life would start to suffer, and eventually my heart would give out. I would hate to be on my deathbed with regrets of working too much and not spending quality time with my family. I couldn't imagine how difficult that would be. So, I challenge you to write this letter pretending the worst happened because you didn't use the discipline the Spirit has given you. And then commit to never forget the importance of sowing seeds of discipline daily in your lives.

The first and best victory is to conquer self.

Plato

Wow, what an emotional roller coaster writing The Letter was. Taking the time to write a letter to my loved ones to read after I died by the fork that fed my flesh was pretty intense and eye opening. My mind is spinning, and I feel like I understand the importance of 1 Corinthians 9:27 now more than ever:

"I discipline my body like an athlete, training it to do what it should. Otherwise, I fear that after preaching to others I myself might be disqualified."

I know the death I wrote about could actually happen if I stop pressing in with the SOULCON lifestyle, if I lose focus on disciplining my body. I know, I could fall to any of the desires to feed my flesh, and for the first time I truly realize my need for men to keep me accountable with walking in the Spirit and not the flesh.

I hear Bugsly call us back into the class, so I grab my letter and head over to the classroom. As I walk down the hall I see some of the other guys walking back toward the classroom. It looks like this challenge hit home with a lot of them. Their eyes are red from tears, and rightfully so. Really engaging in this challenge was extremely emotional. I am sure we will all keep this as a reminder of why it's important to put down our fork and pick up our cross daily.

As we walk into the classroom, we see once again there are no chairs. This time there are yoga mats where the chairs were, so I go stand next to one. In my head I keep thinking the Founder better not be planning to make a group of men do a yoga class! First this emotional letter writing experience, then a chick class? This might be too much in one day.

Commander Bugsly and the Founder greet the class and Bugsly speaks up, "I hope you will never forget the emotions you experienced when you were writing your letter. Please, keep that letter with you and look at it throughout your life. It will help you stay on the SOULCON course with daily living. Writing that letter was one of the most transformational things I have done as a follower of Jesus Christ. Now I'm sure you're wondering why your chairs are missing and replaced with these yoga mats. For that, I will open this part of the lecture up to my good friend and the Founder of SOULCON."

"Thank you Commander! And thank you all for taking this challenge seriously, I believe with all of my heart when Christian men learn how to master their mind, will and emotions, there is no force in the world that can stop them. We have so many men in the Body of Christ with incredible gifts and talents, and most importantly, we all have the Holy Spirit living inside of us! It is our highest responsibility to understand how to walk in the power of the Holy Spirit, and learn how to steward the gifts and talents we have been given.

As soldiers of Jesus Christ we are called to daily sacrifice, daily suffering and all of this with the promise of a joy that no man can take from us. We are called to keep our minds on things in Heaven and not feed the desires of our flesh. And what better way to meditate on that than yoga! Just kidding! Even though I love the benefits of yoga we are not going to do a yoga class. We are going to work on your imagery training. You see one of the things you can control in life, no matter what your external circumstances are, is what you think. The average person thinks 30,000 to 50,000 thoughts a day, but only you can select the thoughts you want to dwell on. Only you can focus your mind and fill your brain with good. We are going to do a quick challenge, then I am going to share something I learned during my time serving this great country. Remember this challenge today, like this training center is about pushing your body to do something so you can learn to identify the pain and overcome it with your mind, will and emotions. We are going to practice this with a plank challenge. You're going to have a challenge with the members on your team to see who can hold a plank the longest. Remember, identify the pain, and overcome! Let's get started…"

DAILY CHALLENGE

Today for your prayer time, focus on praying for your teammates going through this challenge with you...while you do the plank. Make sure everyone on the team does the plank challenge with you today. Just identify the pain of the plank, and overcome it with praying for your team. Keep your time and see who can hold the plank the longest without dropping to the floor. Kick butt!

And now, dear brothers and sisters, one final thing. Fix your thoughts on what is true, and honorable, and right, and pure, and lovely, and admirable. Think about things that are excellent and worthy of praise.

Philippians 4:8 (NLT)

After the plank challenge (that I proudly took third with a time of 3 minutes and 23 seconds) the Founder continues,

"Congratulations on completing the plank challenge! Just like the challenges you have done so far, you experienced what you thought was your breaking point. But please know, we have no idea how capable we truly are... I challenge you to always focus on this thought; you are more capable and stronger than you know. Never be satisfied with what you've accomplished, take some time to enjoy it, but focus on learning ways to constantly improve yourself, your attitude, your emotional and your physical state. This will allow you to remember, as Christians, we are called to following a perfect Savior by HIS strength and power and not our own. God's strength, unlike ours, never runs out. When we feel like we can no longer give anything more with our lives, we can think back to the long run, that plank challenge or any other physical challenge during this time and remember how we took control of our minds and soldiered on. We pressed on no matter how loud our flesh was crying out for us to quit. It's in these small moments we gain the confidence to conquer in the defining moments.

I want to read a scripture that you've already covered, one that Bugsly uses teaches on meditation. It's one of my favorites.

'And now, dear brothers and sisters, one final thing. Fix your thoughts on what is true, and honorable, and right, and pure, and lovely, and admirable. Think about things that are excellent and worthy of praise.' Philippians 4:8 (NLT)

The apostle Paul didn't write these words while laying in a hammock on the beach, with his toes in the warm sand. He wrote these words while in prison. He wrote this letting us know how drastically our external circumstances can change, but one thing we can control is our thoughts.

Like Commander Bugsly, I also served in our military. I served for six years and learned many valuable lessons. One of the most important was at a school called SERE. SERE stands for Survival Evasion Resistance and Escape, and in this school I learned so many things. One is that my body can go a little over five days without food. But the most valuable thing I learned in this school was in the last 28 hours during this time where we were tortured like prisoners of war. Torture tactics from loud torturous music while in a small box, to physical torture, to extremely cold weather, we experienced it all. During that time the thing every candidate is supposed to remember is the importance of keeping PMA (positive mental attitude). The instructors taught us in-depth on how our thoughts can change our physiological state during some of the worst times…and they were right. I remember being naked, so cold I couldn't stand it, and thinking about a sunny beach. I remember being hit in the face and thinking about how bad it would hurt if that guy was 7'8" tall instead of only 6'8". I remember playing a round of golf in Maui in my head while I was stuck in a cement box with music playing of a baby crying so loudly I could hardly think. I remember, that PMA stuff… it worked.

So I challenge you, as you continue this journey through this program, never lose your optimism. Never believe the lie that positive thinking isn't for you. Never allow your mind to be conformed by anything. Make sure you submit your mind, will, and emotions to the Spirit every morning. Make sure you never stop learning to live a SOULCON life. I promise, with the activities you have ahead of you and some of the guest speakers you will hear, you will be forever changed by this challenge. Just don't forget what you learned. I look forward to seeing you at graduation!"

DAILY CHALLENGE

Today is a wall-sit challenge. You're going to practice PMA while competing against your team in a wall-sit challenge. Keep your time, and focus on overcoming the feeling of pain with PMA. Push yourself!

And when you fast, don't make it obvious, as the hypocrites do, for they try to look miserable and disheveled so people will admire them for their fasting. I tell you the truth, that is the only reward they will ever get. But when you fast, comb your hair and wash your face. Then no one will notice that you are fasting, except your Father, who knows what you do in private. And your Father, who sees everything, will reward you.

Matthew 6:16-18 (NLT)

Rolling over, I look at the clock…today is the day. Today is the day I have felt a lot of anxiety about. Today is the day our team does a full day of fasting. Personally, I have always hated fasting, and I haven't fasted in years, other than when I'm sleeping. I heard that fast day at the SOULCON Training Center is one that gets everyone completely out of their comfort zone. I know fasting is a great discipline, and I'm learning to love the output of discipline, but the pain of going without even those fluffy egg whites gives me butterflies. Either way, I'm as ready as I can be and I'm thankful I have this group of guys to go through this with me.

I slowly slide out of bed and get on my knees to pray. Just like every morning in this challenge, I pray the Lord's Prayer out loud for my family and team, but today I can sense something different in my spirit. So I sit and quietly wait for the Lord to speak to me. As I'm waiting, I use the imagery training I've learned in the lectures. I picture myself sitting with Jesus in Heaven. And I wait.

Suddenly I feel the presence of the Holy Spirit fill my room. I go from my knees to laying prostrate on the floor, in awe of God's presence. I say out loud to the Lord, "I'm listening Sir." And I wait quietly…

After waiting in God's presence and enjoying the feeling of His presence, He speaks to my heart, "I love you son, please tell everyone about My love."

After He speaks, I feel His presence lift. I just lay there and start praising Him for speaking to me on the day I have been the most intimidated about. Wow, what an encouragement! God is so good.

I slowly stand up, and start getting my clothes ready for the day and head out to the grinder for what I know is going to be a long day. I now have an energy that food cannot give. I haven't heard the Lord speak to my heart like that since I was a young believer.

As I get to the grinder, I see backpacks full of food and boxes full of Gospel tracts. After hearing stories about today, I am ready to find out what's truly in store for us.

Bugsly addresses the class, "Alright team, today is the fast day. No food until tomorrow morning, just water and black coffee. Here at SOULCON every time we focus on fasting, we encourage everyone to focus their energy on loving and giving more than the pain of going without food. And that's what we're going to do today. Each one of you is going to take a backpack full of food and grab 100 Gospel tracts. We're going to walk into the town nearby and we are going to hand food out to anyone who looks hungry. Every time you give food, hand that person a Gospel tract, and listen for the Spirit to speak to your heart. See if the Spirit has anything to say to that person through you. Either way, the focus of this day is giving to and loving people like Jesus. Rather than feeding our hunger we're going to sow seeds for God's Kingdom in this town. Our commitment as men is to leave every place we live or visit better than we found it, and that's only done by sowing seeds of Jesus everywhere, and everyway we can.

So make sure your water bottle is full, since we will walk over 20 miles today. Every time you can, drink water. Staying hydrated is key today. Let's get going!"

DAILY CHALLENGE

Pray for one person today. For example, if you hear someone complain about a headache, ask if you can pray for them. If someone asks you to be praying for someone, stop and pray for that person with the person that asked you. This is not an in your heart prayer, or an "I'll be praying for you" prayer. Today's challenge is to actually pray with someone out loud. Practice being bold with your faith.

No, this is the kind of fasting I want: Free those who are wrongly imprisoned; lighten the burden of those who work for you. Let the oppressed go free, and remove the chains that bind people. Share your food with the hungry, and give shelter to the homeless. Give clothes to those who need them, and do not hide from relatives who need your help. "Then your salvation will come like the dawn, and your wounds will quickly heal. Your godliness will lead you forward, and the glory of the Lord will protect you from behind. Then when you call, the Lord will answer. 'Yes, I am here,' he will quickly reply. "Remove the heavy yoke of oppression. Stop pointing your finger and spreading vicious rumors! Feed the hungry, and help those in trouble. Then your light will shine out from the darkness, and the darkness around you will be as bright as noon. The Lord will guide you continually, giving you water when you are dry and restoring your strength. You will be like a well-watered garden, like an ever-flowing spring. Some of you will rebuild the deserted ruins of your cities. Then you will be known as a rebuilder of walls and a restorer of homes.

Isaiah 58:6-12 (NLT)

I made it! I feel like for the first time in my life I finally understand the purpose and power of fasting. It has always been a discipline I've known was good, but I didn't fully understand it, so I didn't practice it. And honestly going without food is really difficult when your mind is focused on the food you're not eating. However when your mind is focused on being built up in prayer to love and serve others it makes the hunger pangs so much easier to deal with.

I'm excited to meet up with the team for breakfast to talk about yesterday and give God glory for what He did through all of us. As I walk to breakfast, I'm thankful today is the Sabbath Day at SOULCON. My feet are worn out from all of the walking yesterday, and I feel weak from the fast. There is also the looming thought that Hell Week starts tomorrow. But I block that out and focus on enjoying this day and look forward to the end of Hell Week where we all finally get to have a feast day! Praise God!

Walking up to the food in the chow hall egg whites and oatmeal have never smelled so good. I grab my food and head over to the table to sit down with my brothers. Alfred leads the team in a prayer over the food and we all joyfully break the fast as a team.

The excitement from what God did yesterday is almost bubbling out of me so I start the conversation.

"Guys, yesterday was a game changer for me. I have never been so bold with my faith and had such a clear focus for sharing the love of Jesus. I have to be honest, I was more nervous about the evangelism than the fasting, but God shared something with me before the day started that took the anxiety away. After praying for my family and for you guys, the Holy Spirit filled my room with His presence and shared this with me, 'I love you son, please tell everyone about My love.' I know this seems simple for the believer, but knowing the God of the Universe wanted to tell me He loved me, gave me the confidence to talk to anyone about Him yesterday. So as we shared the food and tracts with people, I shared from a full cup of God's love. I will never forget the look in some of those people's eyes when I told them Jesus loves them. What a wonderful experience! I'm so excited we get to take this back to our hometown and impact our community. In one day, our team handed out more than 360 meals and 1,200 Gospel tracts. That's an incredible amount of seeds sown for Jesus! I'm honored to serve Jesus with you guys! For the first time I have realized that God's presence is more satisfying than food."

As I finish talking Alfred speaks up, "Amen brother! I desire more than anything for my wife and now nine-year-old son to see me find more satisfaction in Christ and His work than food. Yesterday was a game changer for me as well. I felt waves of depression come over, the ones I felt when my daughter was fighting for her life in the hospital. But I was able to identify those emotions, submit them to Jesus, and fill my mind with sharing the Good News. To this point, the only thing I have found to overcome those emotions of depression has been focusing all of my energy on worshiping Jesus with my body, soul and spirit. I tried for a long time to find healing in food, but it was always a short-term fix. Worshiping Jesus is truly the only thing that satisfies our souls. Guys, thank you for pushing me and not letting me quit… My mind is being transformed daily and I am learning to submit my emotions…all of them…to Jesus."

As the conversation continues about yesterday I take time to repent to the Lord for not living this lifestyle sooner. I ask God to give me strength to not fall back into the comfortable life I was living before…

As we're all finishing up with breakfast, Commander Bugsly walks into the chow hall.

"Good morning gentlemen. I hope you enjoyed breaking your fast. I am proud of you guys! Seeing your love, passion, and devotion for Jesus inspired me yesterday. Thank you! I want to encourage you to enjoy your Sabbath today. Rest, go to chapel, call home, enjoy your day, because tomorrow is day one of Hell Week. See you at the grinder at 0430!"

DAILY CHALLENGE

Ask the Holy Spirit to fill the room you're in. Take one or two worship songs and ask Him to fill you up so you can pour out for Him. Take 3-5 minutes just worshiping Him in song by yourself. Even if you're like me and can't sing well, that's not a valid excuse. God is worthy of our praise, and if we don't, the rocks will cry out. So set 3-5 minutes aside, turn on some worship music and just focus on God's goodness. Ask the Spirit to move in your life.

WEEK 03 RESULTS

Be sure to share your results and encourage others
going through the challenge on the SOULCON App.

WEEK 03 REFLECTIONS

Be sure to share your reflections and encourage others
going through the challenge on the SOULCON App.

THE SOULCON CHALLENGE OBJECTIVES:

- Pray the Lord's Prayer out loud, on your knees – EVERY DAY
- No carbs after 3pm from grains and breads (sweet potatoes, vegetables, and berries are the only carbs you can have).
    - Track your caloric intake in the book or on an app, just record everything except for your three feast days.
- Drink at least 64oz of water a day
- Exercise at least 30 minutes 5 days a week
    - Run, walk or crawl, two 5ks (3.1 miles) a week
- Before you leave home for the day do 40 push-ups (or as many as you can)
- Sleep 6-8 hours a night (excluding feast days)
- Evangelism: Hand out a total of ten Gospel tracts to people you don't know.

If you're going through hell, keep going.

Winston Churchill

As Tyler, Alfred and I jog up to the grinder we are all a little anxious. Our whole team is there right at 0430 but there's no sight of Commander Bugsly. This is the first time he hasn't been out there right on time with our team. Something is up...

Our team starts joking about the possibility of Bugsly sleeping in. It's about 0435 and guns start to go off. There are three silhouettes running toward us, and they are all firing what sounds like AK-47s in the air. One of the voices scream, "Get on the deck! Get in the push-up position!" Our team hits the deck...

These three guys start walking between everyone, shooting their guns in the air.

"What in the world is this?! What does this week have in store?!" I say to Tyler as we get into the push-up position.

At that point, Commander Bugsly begins to speak, "Good morning team! Today marks the first of six full days of learning to not quit while walking through hell on this earth. Our goal as instructors is to show you that you're stronger than you know, you're stronger than you feel, and you can accomplish more than you ever thought was possible. This week you're going to be pushed, you're going to compete against each other, and at the end, you will celebrate with an entire day of feasting! But this week will not end until you all realize the goal of this program. We are training you as elite soldiers of Jesus Christ to know you're saved, and then to have the courage to ask Him to send you into the hells of this earth. This week will teach you how to mentally overcome the hell of pains in your body with the hopes that you will remember this when the real spiritual attacks come. Gentlemen, in Christ you are stronger than you know. We are going to help you see that this week."

Bugsly is one intense dude. But I am thankful he takes this so seriously. For the record, I am seriously looking forward to our feast day. I think that thought alone is going to help me take on any challenge this week. This is hands down the longest I've been without allowing myself to overeat on sweets, and I'm pretty proud of that. I look forward to what's on the other end of this week, but now it's time to experience it.

Sitting here in the push-up position I begin to think about my family back home. About how this is going to make me a better husband and father...that thought gives me the energy to smile in the face of this upcoming pain. I am actually learning to embrace pain.

Bugsly yells out to the class, "Knock out a quick 75 push-ups and get ready for your first challenge of the day." We all, surprisingly, finish the push-ups and stand up for the next instructions.

"The first challenge is a 10 mile team run. Your goal isn't time, but it's finishing with everyone on your team. If you have someone quit running, you all fail. And failure this week means push-ups, sit-ups and squats. This week is all about accountability. This life as a believer would be easy if the enemy came at us with AK-47s like this morning. But satan and his demons come at us subtly. They come at us with the fork that feeds our flesh, tiny little bites that don't seem deadly, and this week we are going to learn how to destroy that fork every day by picking up our cross and submitting to the Spirit. Trust me gentlemen, for the next six days you're going to have to use the strength of the Spirit. It's going to push you to your limit...and then a little further. Let's get ready to run, the other instructors and I will be running behind you, making sure you don't fail. Remember the only failure on this run is if someone stops running. So stay encouraged, and finish strong!"

DAILY CHALLENGE

Use your exercise time today to focus on the importance of not quitting. Add on an extra mile to your workout today and don't worry about the speed, just focus on finishing. Identify the temptation to quit and overcome it with a positive mental attitude (PMA).

Don't you realize that in a race everyone runs, but only one person gets the prize? So run to win! All athletes are disciplined in their training. They do it to win a prize that will fade away, but we do it for an eternal prize. So I run with purpose in every step. I am not just shadowboxing. I discipline my body like an athlete, training it to do what it should. Otherwise, I fear that after preaching to others I myself might be disqualified.

1 Corinthians 9:24-27 (NIV)

As our team successfully crosses the finish line of the 10-mile run, we all celebrate. We did it! The joy of being a finisher is on everyone's face and confidence is exuding from the team. We all get to take a break for water and then jog over to the chow hall.

As we're jogging to the chow hall I think about the verse in 1 Corinthians 9:24. I have never thought about it like Bugsly explained it on the run. Bugsly said running to win in the Body of Christ is focusing on helping others win.

One thing I love about the team runs is how Commander Bugsly will teach us from the Bible right in the middle of the run. And this morning he did it from one of the best passages in the Bible on discipline. For the first time I now view that passage as one of service and not vain competition. Bugsly said on the run that the only way we can win as followers of Christ is by loving God and serving others…period. This passage now comes to life in a new way for me. On that 10-mile run the only way the team would win is if everyone finished. I take that thought and think about how it applies with my family and loved ones back home. The realization that life isn't a solo sprint, but a team run where encouragement and accountability are crucial to winning fills my mind.

Bugsly said, "When we're strong and when we're tired, we have to keep our focus on Jesus who finished strong, and ran His race perfectly."

Bugsly also quoted Hebrews 12:1-3 on our run from The Message translation and told our team to use our imagination with this while we run in the future or whenever we need motivation:

"Do you see what this means—all these pioneers who blazed the way, all these veterans cheering us on? It means we'd better get on with it. Strip down, start running—and never quit! No extra spiritual fat, no parasitic sins. Keep your eyes on Jesus, who both began and finished this race we're in. Study how he did it. Because he never lost sight of where he was headed—that exhilarating finish in and with God—he could put up with anything along the way: Cross, shame, whatever. And now he's there, in the place of honor, right alongside God. When you find yourselves flagging in your faith, go over that story again, item by item, that long litany of hostility he plowed through. That will shoot adrenaline into your souls!"

This whole time at the SOULCON Training Center I'm learning Jesus is the one who keeps us motivated, Jesus is the one who helps us, and Jesus is the one who will satisfy our every need. I'm learning how along this race of life that the more I know and follow Jesus, the more I can become like Jesus to others.

As we all walk into the chow hall we realize there is no oatmeal or bread, I totally forgot that a part of Hell Week means there are no carbohydrates other than from fruit, veggies and legumes. Just thinking about how good a bowl of oatmeal would be after that run makes my mouth water… But I thank God for the food we have, I grab some egg whites and fruit, and walk over to grab a cup of coffee.

Our team all sits down together as always and prays.

This time Tyler leads the team in a prayer, "God thank you for showing us that you are more satisfying than anything in this world. Thank you for this training center to train us to live with our soul in control by Your Spirit and not our flesh. As we eat this food Jesus we do it to glorify you, as we do this week we ask that we learn how capable you've made us, and we ask that you give us the strength to learn the joy in persevering through pain, amen."

Commander Bugsly walks in with that AK-47 strapped around his back…goofy guy. He gives us all a greeting and encourages our class. He tells us where to meet for the next challenge, and reminds us to bring our swim trunks. I take another sip of my coffee, and smile.

"No matter what is ahead, bring it on." I say to the team. We all finish our breakfast and head out of the chow hall a little anxious for the next challenge.

DAILY CHALLENGE

Take time in your day to encourage someone. Be very specific. Make sure it's not just something in passing; make sure it's a blessing to that person. Write a note, pay for their coffee, or do something to show that person how much you appreciate them. Learn from Commander Bugsly in how he highlighted the only way to truly win in our race is to help others win. Be intentional about being an encouragement today.

If you do not conquer self, you will be conquered by self.
Napoleon Hill

After running back to our room to grab our swim trunks, our team is on our way down to the water-training center for the next challenge. I have heard about the training we're about to endure, and I'm not that excited about it.

As we walk into the water-training center there is a big above ground pool full of ice, we see Commander Bugsly behind the pool with a big smile on his face. I look around at everyone on the team and we all grimace because we know this is going to hurt. As we walk up, Bugsly directs us to line up and get ready to walk into the tub.

He prays, "Father God, I ask you allow these men to learn from Your Spirit during this time. I ask that You teach them the importance of accountability, and the importance of keeping their thoughts on You during every circumstance they face. Father, I ask You continue to help these men mature as followers of Your Son, in Jesus name we pray and live, amen."

Bugsly continues, "Okay men, it's time to test your mental strength. This whole training center is focused on submitting your mind, will, and emotions to the Holy Spirit and not to your flesh. Throughout this course we have taught there is a daily battle between the flesh and the Spirit to gain control over your soul, and that as men it's imperative to live everyday yielded to the Spirit. This next challenge will help you all identify the voice of your flesh so you can learn to overcome it by submitting to the Spirit. You are going to take your shirts off so you're just in your swim trunks, and you're going to get in the ice tub, together. In this tub you will learn quickly that if you stay together it's easier than if you're alone. Remember that truth the rest of your life. You will also learn the power of controlling your mind. Focus your mind on heaven like Colossians 3:2 says:

'Think about the things of heaven, not the things of earth.'

So no matter how cold you get, use your mind to put you in a different place. Use your mind to put you sitting with Jesus in Heaven, where it's warm and suffering is a vague memory. Learning to do this is crucial to the success of your life as an elite soldier of Jesus."

All right, here it goes. We all have to get in the ice bath, and once we are all in, we have to stand in the water and ice for 10 minutes together. If anyone gets out, we have to do it again tomorrow, and we are all committed to only experiencing this joy once.

We all start moving forward. I take my first step in the water and thoughts race through my head that this water will eventually be above my waist...that's a miserable thought. Everyone starts laughing and joking to take their mind off the pain.

Okay, we're in, and up to our chests in this ice water. A wave of emotions runs through my head about how this is going to be impossible to take it 10 minutes. It feels like everything in me is going crazy, panic is starting to set in, I can feel my mind screaming to quit. All I can think about is a warm cup of coffee, my body is shaking uncontrollably. I literally feel like this might kill me...I don't think I can take this.

Just then Tyler comes over and puts his arm around me.

"Easy princess, just breathe, it will be over soon and then you can go back and fix your make-up." Even in this freezing cold, miserable water, Tyler has enough in him to give me a hard time. But his words were enough to calm me down and help the feeling of panic to subside. I look around and I can see some of the guys are panicking like me, and some are smiling.

Tyler tells us, "Let's bring it in guys, remember accountability will help us finish strong."

With that, the team gathers in a tight circle, and everyone locks their arms together, braced to finish this challenge strong. I look up at the clock above Bugsly's head, thinking it has to be close to halfway over, but the clock says 1:23 and it is going up to 10:00. This might be a little more difficult than I thought.

Bugsly starts to instruct the class, "This is something you can practice the rest of your life. It's always good to get out of your comfort zone and practice being uncomfortable. Christ has called us to live as a sacrifice for Him, so we have to embrace discomforts along the journey of living in service to others. Living as a sacrifice of service will always be challenging, and it will have pain, just remember true growth is impossible without pain. So embrace it and learn as much as you can from it."

I feel my body start to shake uncontrollably and I feel a wave of panic come over me. There has only been three minutes that have passed and I feel like I can't make it. I have been working on believing that I truly can do all things through Christ like Philippians 4:13 says, so I start saying it out loud to myself quietly. Alfred hears me and recognizes that I'm struggling at the moment, so he shares a joke with the team.

"A friend was in front of me coming out of church one day, and the preacher was standing at the door as he always is to shake hands. He grabbed my friend by the hand and pulled him aside. The Pastor said to him, 'You need to join the Army of the Lord!' My friend replied, 'I'm already in the Army of the Lord, Pastor.' The Pastor replied, 'How come I don't see you except at Christmas and Easter?' My friend whispered back, 'Because I'm in the secret service.'"

His ability to laugh and joke really helps the morale of the team.

Then Tyler starts, "Remember how the Apostle Paul would worship God when he was chained up and in prison? He was such a stud! Let's learn from him and sing a worship song together, we can practice suffering well."

So Tyler leads the team in Amazing Grace. As I start singing I realize the pain subsides and my mind is more focused on praising God than the suffering of the external circumstance. I look back up at the clock and see 8:58. We're almost there. I think our bodies are completely numb at this point, so I think we will make it. I start to reflect on the control I am learning over my body. I can remember times after stressful days back home, when I would feel like my body was in complete control and I would pull off the road and grab a fast food value meal. I remember the feeling of discouragement I would feel over my lack of self-control. But now, watch out! I am learning to live in the power of the Holy Spirit in the face of these crazy external pressures. What an incredible time in the Lord this has been...

Bugsly yells, "You made it! Great job guys! Be careful getting out, don't trust your legs too much at this point."

That had to be one of the longest 10 minutes of my life, but our whole team made it. I realized there are times when God remains quiet when we are going through challenges, and tests, and when that happens we have to stand, we have to be strong in His Word, and wait for the storm to pass. What valuable lessons our team learned today from freezing our butts off...

DAILY CHALLENGE

During your shower time today, turn the water to cold for two minutes. Do your best to hear the voice of your flesh and overcome it. Use some of the tactics the team used in the ice bath training. This is a great practice to work on mental toughness. Good luck and enjoy that coffee once you're done.

For we must all stand before Christ to be judged. We will each receive whatever we deserve for the good or evil we have done in this earthly body.

2 Corinthians 5:10 (NLT)

After sitting in that ice bath, a cup of black coffee never tasted so good. We are all extremely grateful to be finished with that challenge and thankful to be in our chairs in the classroom in warm, dry, clothes.

We are all still talking about the ice bath and the writing on the board catches my eye, XXX. My heart sinks when I realize what we're about to discuss. Just then Bugsly walks in, shuts the door, and begins the lecture:

"First off, great job in the ice bath team! You guys did great, and Tyler, great job leading the team in worship during that time. You helped everyone pass over three minutes. Well done!

Now since we're in Hell Week, let's dive into two areas where the kingdom of darkness is advancing in the lives of the men in the Body of Christ, porn and gluttony.

I know these are sensitive issues, but if we don't address them, who will? Let me say before we begin, the ground is even at the foot of the cross. So if you are struggling with one of these, it's time to man up and confess it to one of your teammates. You know in your heart if you are, and if you are, by the end of this talk we will have a confession time with the group and then a time of prayer. It takes a man to confess and repent, so don't be embarrassed. We have to be vulnerable with each other or the enemy will get a foothold in our lives and destroy us. Remember, he hates us and wants us dead.

So as you progress through SOULCON, you are learning about your soul and how it functions. You're learning the voice of your soul (mind, will and emotions) and you're learning the importance of submitting your soul to the Spirit every day. There are desires that are good in your life like sex, eating, sleeping, relaxing etc. Desires that are God given, but desires that have boundaries and need to be exercised in the control of the Holy Spirit. But if you have an inordinate desire for those things they become out of control, and deadly. Two of those areas we're going to address today are sex and eating.

Sex, as we know is something God designed as a wonderful thing for a human, but its intention is for a man and a woman to enjoy it in the confines of the marriage covenant. Your desire to have sex was never intended to be fulfilled by videos of women on your computer, tablet or phone, and then carried out with masturbation. God has designed your body to be your wife's for sexual fulfillment and you do not have free reign over your body. Everything we do in these bodies we will give an account for, and satan and his demons are on a mission to steal, kill and destroy every part of your life.

I want to challenge you, if you are feeding your flesh with fork size bites of pornography; please confess to the Lord and your team. Confess and repent from the porn, if you don't it will snowball and cause destruction in some area of your life."

I couldn't stand it anymore, and I had to raise my hand…

"Guys, I have to confess. I have a great marriage and I love my wife like crazy. But sometimes my desire for sex gets out of control. I find myself turning to my phone where she doesn't know what I look at; I masturbate and then don't confess my sin with anyone. I haven't even told my best friend Tyler. I just keep it to myself. But I have learned here at SOULCON that the Spirit is more satisfying than the fork that feeds my flesh in every area. So please pray for me, and hold me accountable. As of today, I confess to you all and I repent."

As I said that, I felt a weight lift off my back, finally, freedom. Three other guys in the class confess as well. Commander Bugsly has the class gather around me and the other three guys, and the class prays for us. For the first time in years I feel a peace in my heart and mind in this area. Tears come to my eyes and I thank the guys on this team.

"I love and appreciate you guys!"

"We love you too brother!" Gage says back to me.

"Alright guys, great job," Bugsly says, "just make sure you put barriers on those phones and devices to guard yourselves against times when you're weak. It's important to understand it's easier to remove a temptation when you're strong than try to overcome a temptation when you're weak. Now we're going to cover gluttony. This is just as dangerous as pornography. As a matter of fact, gluttony is killing more people right now than it ever has in the history of the world. At this training center we encourage feasting and fasting, but never gluttony. Gluttony is when you cannot control your body, and you overeat. This as a SOULCON soldier is always forgivable, like any sin, but it should never be tolerated, like any sin. Gluttony is something that has to stop with us. If we don't commit to being change agents, it will destroy the health of the hearts, minds and bodies of the Church. Men, we have to lead. If we do, our families and our churches will follow our leadership. We can no longer allow gluttony to overtake us. How many of you will commit today to not surrender to this control anymore? To walk in constant accountability with this?"

Everyone in the class raises their hands, and we all pray together. What a challenging day this has been so far. Good, but challenging.

But if we confess our sins to him, he is faithful and just to forgive us our sins and to cleanse us from all wickedness.
1 John 1:9 (NLT)

DAILY CHALLENGE

Are you struggling with porn? If so, call, text or email one of the guys on your team and confess it to them. Repent to the Lord and ask the Holy Spirit for help to never be controlled by your flesh in this area again. Then set up boundaries on your phone, tablet and computer. Get porn blockers on your devices.

What about gluttony? If so, do the same thing. Confess and repent. Ask for accountability with these areas and set up boundaries to protect yourself.

Let each man find out what God wants him to do, and then let him do it, or die in the attempt.

Charles Spurgeon

After a long day yesterday, I'm ready for day two of this challenging week. I can almost taste the sweet food I'm going to devour on the feast day. Thankfully our team has a break from running this morning, I just hope that's not a bad thing since it is Hell Week.

After we finished breakfast, I think we are all starting to embrace that being hungry is a part of this week, and we all feel confident we're ready for whatever Commander Bugsly has in store for us. I mean, we killed the challenges yesterday, I don't think we will face anything else as challenging mentally as the ice bath…I hope.

As we walk into the classroom for the lecture, there are spin bikes where our chairs should be. Commander Bugsly is up at the front with that familiar smirk on his face.

"Go ahead gentlemen," Bugsly says, "Grab a seat. Make sure the seat is adjusted properly for your height and then strap your feet in. This class is going to have a race today, a race to see who can get the most miles during the course of our lectures. If you are one of the top three winners you will get to have a one-hour video call with your family tonight. If you take last place, you will be the one cleaning the sweat off the floor once the class is dismissed tonight, and trust me, with how much sweat will be poured, you don't want to be in last place."

Tyler looks over at me and gives me his usual optimistic smile. This incentive to take top three is pretty incredible. With the lack of reception here a phone call is the only thing we have had with our families, so to see them and talk to them would mean the world to all of us. I bet the competition is going to be pretty strong today. I just wish I could have some oatmeal. But mind over matter right?

"We've got this brother!" I say to Tyler as I adjust the bike for my height. Each bike is hooked up to the computer next to it and then to the projector at the front so everyone can see each other's progress. There's no opportunity to slack off today, if anyone does, the whole class will see it. This positive peer pressure thing is no joke...

Commander Bugsly starts speaking to the class about the importance of being all in for Jesus. He shares from his time in the military, and how there were so many men he served with who gave their lives for this country. They went through some of the most difficult training in the world, they lived without a great paycheck, they traveled all of the time, and then their lives ended up being one of a sacrifice for this country.

As Commander Bugsly is teaching, the thoughts are going through my head of how little effort I give in my life as a Christ follower. I have not trained like I should, and honestly I have been lazy in memorizing scripture, my prayer time, and my spiritual leadership in our home. I'm learning this isn't something that happens naturally or comfortably in a relationship with Jesus. These spiritual disciplines take effort, and consistency. As I sit on the bike and push myself hard with the hopes of having a video call home, I can't help but think of how my muscles, bones, heart, and brain are being developed by riding this bike. This bike is a great workout, but dang, this seat is a little invasive.

I have to focus my mind on the lecture and the end reward more than the momentary pain.

"Pain is temporary," I say quietly to myself, "push on!"

At SOULCON they teach that by only having certain allotted times to call home it's an opportunity to train your mind and heart to focus solely on the Spirit and on your relationship with Him. This training center takes leading our families very seriously and they constantly remind the teams how men can never disconnect from the Spirit or it will impact their entire lives. I'm very thankful for this and everything this program is doing in my life, but I can't stop thinking about how nice it would be to see my family on a video call. That gives me the wind in my sails to push a little harder and faster.

As the day winds down, our class continues to race one another before the clock hits five o'clock. Once it does, the time is up. Currently Tyler, Gage and I are in the top three. None of us have taken a break all day when we could, we just pressed on. As the clock hit five we all rejoiced that it was over. I am filled with joy as we celebrate because I am one of the top three. Praise God! I didn't think I could keep pushing myself all day, but I did! That's a big victory for me. As I look at the board I see Alfred took last by a long shot, so he has to clean the room. To my surprise the whole team stays and helps Alfred clean. The team has such a love for Alfred, this guy has been through more than a man should have to endure.

As we're cleaning I feel the Holy Spirit soften my heart and prompt me to give my video call to Alfred.

"Yes sir," I say to the Lord, "I would be honored to." So I walk over to him and give my call to him. Tears fill his eyes and he gives me a big, sweaty bear hug.

"I cannot tell you how much this means to me brother! I needed this more than you know... I love you man, thank you!"

What an incredible feeling...it truly is better to give than receive.

"You should remember the words of the Lord Jesus: 'It is more blessed to give than to receive.'" Acts 20:35b

DAILY CHALLENGE

Learning to give our best to the Lord and others is one of the best lessons we can learn. Your challenge today is to give someone a gift. It can be money, a favorite book, a possession or anything of value to you. Do this in hope of encouraging this person in the Lord or maybe introducing this person to the Lord for the first time.

Greater love has no one than this, than to lay down one's life for his friends.

John 15:13 (NKJV)

After an incredibly challenging week we have all made it to the last day of the SOULCON Hell Week. This is very rare. There are usually one or two guys that call it quits from the challenge during this week. It's hard, but this team has learned to focus their minds and emotions on the eternal reward of this training more than the momentary pain of discipline.

This SOULCON life is now a part of who I am. I have learned more about myself and my appetite for anything other than Jesus this week than I have at any time in my Christian life. I had no idea just by cutting certain foods out of my diet, walking in such transparent accountability with other men, and doing an incredible amount of cardiovascular training that I would run into such deep-rooted barriers to my intimacy with Christ. From confessing my struggle with occasional pornography with the guys on this team, to learning to depend on their strength and presence in the ice bath training, this week has been life changing. And there's still one more day...

After our morning 5k run with the team, which was a little slower than the other ones because we are all hungry and sore, we are ready for our healthy breakfast with no carbs other than fruit. Man, that feast day is calling my name. I see visions of donuts running through my head.

After breakfast we all head over to the classroom ready for whatever challenge is next. There's a sharply dressed man at the front standing next to Commander Bugsly. As we take our seats, we are eager to hear what this guy's story is and what he has to share with our class.

Commander Bugsly opens up, "Good morning team! Great run this morning! You have all done amazing this week! Please give yourselves a pat on the back. I'm very proud of you. Obviously, today is the last day of Hell Week and the day before your first feast day, but in my opinion our next speaker is going to bring us the most important message of Hell Week. He is an extremely successful businessman and one of the wealthiest men in this region. He is going to share with you a lesson from what he considers to be the worst failure of his life."

As Bugsly finishes, the sharp dressed man, and the only guy in a suit on the SOULCON campus begins to address the class, "Good morning! I count it an honor to be here with your team and be privileged to be a speaker in this great program. I hope and pray what I am going to share with you will encourage your heart to never lose sight of the most important gift God will ever give you.

As Bugsly said, I am a successful businessman and I am very wealthy, but it wasn't without cost. Twenty-two years ago, I started a business with a dream and a solid plan. The business I started was all consuming and if it was going to make it, it was going to take a lot of hard work, strategic planning and constant networking. I will never forget how many hardships I went through during the start of this business, I must have heard 'you can't make it' hundreds of times. But I kept plugging along. Most weeks for the first two years I would work seven days a week for at least twelve hours each day. I was young, I had passion and energy, but no idea I had a deep struggle with putting work before my relationship with God and the incredible wife he had blessed me with. But I'm a guy, and I was focused on the thrill of chasing my dream rather than pursuing Jesus and the wife He had given me. I remember hearing complaints from my wife in the first few years about her lack of attention from me, and not feeling like I was pursuing her. It just annoyed me and made me feel disrespected. I felt like she didn't appreciate the hard work I was putting into a business to provide for our future family. So I kept on building this business and chasing the dream in my heart even though I missed church most weekends and my wife's emotions were constantly left on E.

After seven years of long days and constant labor, I had made my business into a million dollar entity and I was being recognized as one of the most successful men in the city. I will never forget going to those events with my wife. I was so thrilled and honored, and I would get hurt when she wasn't ecstatic for my successes. Our family at the time had grown by two, a son and daughter, and we could do just about anything we wanted financially. In my head things were great. But I will never forget when everything changed.

I came home from a trip, where I had just acquired a great new business entity, to a note on the table and an empty house. My wife was leaving me. It was horrifying. I hit my knees and cried out to God. It was honestly the first time I had been on my knees since I started my business. I remember asking God to help, and promising that I would do anything to get my family back. God answered me that day. He did help me, He helped me endure the pain of divorce. And I believe that is a strength only God can give.

I remember for an entire year I refocused my life, and my business. I reconnected with Jesus as my Savior, my best friend, and the Lord of my life and business. I worked at being friends with my wife and a present dad to the children wounded by my actions, or lack of actions that led to divorce. And God is faithful...

I stand before you today a restored man, a refocused man, and a man proud to say God can truly turn any situation around. After five years I remarried my wife and I don't let one day pass where I do not pursue Jesus, her, and my kids more than I do my business.

I remember coming through this program and learning what it is to be a true disciple of Jesus and learning to live my life out of my priorities and not my external pressures. I learned the importance of living with my soul in control by the Holy Spirit and not my flesh. I am proud to tell you the stronghold of being a workaholic is broken over my life. I practice the SOULCON lifestyle weekly to make sure I don't fall back into a life led by the flesh instead of a life led by the Spirit. I promise, and please hear me, the peace God gives is more satisfying than any amount of money or success can give you. The peace God gives allows you to finish your race strong and whole spiritually. Stay in His peace, and if you walk out of it, run back to it. Nothing is more satisfying.

I hope and pray you take what you learn here and live it the rest of your life. It's only in walking with the Spirit daily that we as humans find true success. Thank you for your time, and I leave you with my favorite passage of scripture and a challenge to live this daily in your life:

For a husband is the head of his wife as Christ is the head of the church. He is the Savior of his body, the church. As the church submits to Christ, so your wives should submit to your husbands in everything. For husbands, this means love your wives, just as Christ loved the church. He gave up his life for her to make her holy and clean, washed by the cleansing of God's word. He did this to present her to himself as a glorious church without a spot or wrinkle or any other blemish. Instead, she will be holy and without fault. In the same way, husbands ought to love their wives as they love their own bodies. For a man who loves his wife actually shows love for himself. No one hates his own body but feeds and cares for it, just as Christ cares for the church. And we are members of his body." Ephesians 5:23-30 (NLT)

DAILY CHALLENGE

If you are married, do one thing to pursue your wife today. Go out of your way to write her a note, buy her some flowers, or just text her and let her know you love her and five reasons why you love her. If you're single, write a note to the Lord highlighting five things you love the most about Him. Be specific.

Then he said to them, 'Go your way, eat the fat, drink the sweet, and send portions to those for whom nothing is prepared; for this day is holy to our Lord. Do not sorrow, for the joy of the Lord is your strength.'

Nehemiah 8:10 (NKJV)

Wow… This has been one heck of a ride. As I lay here in my bed, I look at the clock and see 0721. All I can do is praise God for making one day a week to be a Sabbath. Taking a Sabbath and making it a priority is one of the best disciplines I have learned so far in SOULCON. This has been something taught over and over at this training center, and honestly, it's one of my weakest areas. There have been so many times I have hurt my family by deciding to work through the weekend, or all the times when I didn't take the time to sit back and smell the roses and just enjoy life. As hard as SOULCON pushes all of us, every one of the instructors pushes us to have fun just as much. Some of the instructors here say having fun that honors Christ is one of the best disciplines in a Godly home. And having been a serious, constantly driven workaholic, I completely agree with that and needed that teaching.

Even though our team has had days to give our bodies rest over the past four weeks, this is the first day we get to give our healthy eating a rest. And after Hell Week we are all ready. Today is our team's first feast day! Praise God! I have so many foods running through my head that I'm excited to eat. I'm so pumped because the first stop for our team is to a local donut shop by the training center. I have been craving those donuts the whole time we've been here. Every once in a while on the morning runs, when the wind is blowing from east to west our team can smell the fresh donuts being made. And no matter how filling egg whites and oatmeal are, they will never smell as good as those donuts. It brings so much joy to my heart to know today is the day we get to feast!

After an easy morning I head over to meet up with the guys, and everyone looks refreshed and ready to eat. We hop in the

SOULCON van and head over to the shop. As we walk in, I see the beautiful assortment of donuts and the wave of delightful smells fill my nose. I almost feel like I can just sit here and smell the donuts without having to eat them because of the fantastic aroma. But for the record, that would be crazy, it's time to eat. Before I came to this training center I would have easily walked into a shop like this and bought a dozen, and had at least four of them before they made it back to the house. But not today, I'm just going to order my two favorites. My goal is to enjoy the food and not lose control. The whole purpose of this training is to live a SOULCON lifestyle, even on feast days.

As we all sit down, we pray and thank God for this amazing food. After the prayer, I sink my teeth into the first bite of a sweet, fatty food in four weeks…and it tastes AMAZING! I can see why healthy eating is a discipline, and this is a delight. So many memories flood my brain on how this flavor "high" used to have a control over me. Foods like these would constantly be ringing in my head, tempting me to overeat junk food when I knew I wasn't supposed to.

What Commander Bugsly always says about taking a feast day comes to my mind:

"Life without feasting is like marriage without sex."

That Bugsly is a pretty incredible guy. He is truly a guy who focuses on living in SOULCON every day. It's exciting to think this SOULCON lifestyle is something I am going to live everyday when I am back with my family in our hometown. I hope I can be an inspiration to someone like Commander Bugsly has been to me. I actually feel for the first time in my life that I have control over my health. I know it's because I'm committing every area of my life to be controlled by the Spirit…even with my feasting. Praise God!

I'm ready to feast and rest for the remainder of the day, then tomorrow it's back at it!

Therefore, whether you eat or drink, or whatever you do, do all to the glory of God.
                                        1 Corinthians 10:31 (NKJV)

DAILY CHALLENGE

Congratulations! You made it! Your challenge today is to feast without losing control. Enjoy the delicious foods you have been fasting from, just make sure you're stilling living SOULCON.

WEEK 04 RESULTS

Be sure to share your results and encourage others
going through the challenge on the SOULCON App.

WEEK 04 REFLECTIONS

Be sure to share your reflections and encourage others
going through the challenge on the SOULCON App.

THE SOULCON CHALLENGE OBJECTIVES:

- Pray the Lord's Prayer out loud, on your knees – EVERY DAY
- No carbs after 3pm from grains and breads (sweet potatoes, vegetables, and berries are the only carbs you can have).
  - Track your caloric intake in the book or on an app, just record everything except for your three feast days.
- Drink at least 64oz of water a day
- Exercise at least 30 minutes 5 days a week
  - Run, walk or crawl, two 5ks (3.1 miles) a week
- Before you leave home for the day do 40 push-ups (or as many as you can)
- Sleep 6-8 hours a night (excluding feast days)
- Evangelism: Hand out a total of ten Gospel tracts to people you don't know.

Dear friends, I urge you, as foreigners and exiles, to abstain from sinful desires, which wage war against your soul.

1 Peter 2:11 (NIV)

"Good morning gentlemen!" Bugsly says as our team sits down for our first lecture of our second Max Week, week five. "I hope you all had a great feast day! I don't think I have looked as forward to sweet and fatty foods as I did after the Hell Week I went through at this training center. What a great day that was! It's a monumental day for a majority of the people who come through this program. It helps all of us learn how to enjoy food without losing control. This is something we can learn with our eating as well as every area of our flesh, and this brings us into today's topic. Today's topic is a difficult one, but it's a topic everyone at SOULCON feels very passionate about addressing. Though we have touched on it before, today we are going to dive in deeper. The topic is what we call the Elephant in the Room in every men's group, the topic is masturbation.

In most groups of men this is a topic rarely discussed because it is an extremely challenging as well as personal issue. But here at the SOULCON Training Center we look at every person as a brother that comes through this program, and as brothers, we have to talk about and confront the challenging and personal topics. Because in the end, our goal here is to better equip every man going through this program to start every day, and finish every day walking and living with their soul in control by the Holy Spirit. So if we have areas where we are walking in the flesh, they need to be addressed, and masturbation can be one of the areas most men view as an acceptable feeding of the flesh. Gentlemen, there are no bites that we take from the fork that feeds our flesh that will not bring destruction in our lives. Every area where your flesh desires to be fed is an area where we could be tempted to step out of the power of the Spirit. And that is a scary place to be. Like the Apostle Peter said under the power of the Spirit in 1 Peter 2:11:

'Dear friends, I urge you, as foreigners and exiles, to abstain from sinful desires, which wage war against your soul.'

It's crucial for us to understand and know the power of walking in the flesh and walking in the Spirit in every area of our lives. So we have to be on guard against the attacks of the enemy, and his secret weapon in the lives of followers of Jesus is the fork that feeds our flesh. So let's talk about two things every man needs to cover with the topic of masturbation:

- Are my actions pleasing to the Lord?
- Is my spouse, my closest accountability partner comfortable with my actions?

These are two questions that will help you personally discover if masturbation is a sin in your life or not. The Bible never confronts this head on. There are multiple scriptures talking about the importance of keeping a pure heart and walking in accountability with our actions to the Lord, and our spouses or future spouses. So if you can look at masturbation with a pure heart, and feel comfortable talking with God about your actions, then in my opinion, as your instructor, it's not sinful. I believe there are absolutely cases like this. God knows our weakness and our need for orgasms. God made us as men, full of testosterone, and He also knows our wives don't want or need sex as much as we do. God knows being man is hard, Jesus lived in a body just like us, He felt temptation and He never gave in. Jesus relates with us and He never looks down and condemns us for making mistakes, but He has given us His Spirit to help us get back up when we fall. We can never forget the same Holy Spirit that lived in Jesus lives in us; therefore we have the power to walk in purity. That is why living in SOULCON is of the highest importance in our lives.

Men, we have to make sure we never become numb to the dangers of feeding our flesh, married or single, it's our duty to honor God with our bodies. It's our duty to take the purity of our heart seriously. So if you're masturbating and you start to use your deep thoughts to lust after another woman, or any visual stimulation (other than a picture of your wife), then it's sinful and destructive to the purity of our hearts and minds. Our actions can only be pleasing to God if they line up with scripture and in Matthew 5:28 Jesus says:

'But I say to you that whoever looks at a woman to lust for her has already committed adultery with her in his heart.' (NKJV)

So if looking at a woman with lust in your eyes is adultery, surely masturbating while visualizing her having sex with you is adultery. So guard against it! Your soul (mind, will and emotions) has a war for its dominion. Everyday your flesh wants to control your soul, and so does the Spirit, but you have to choose. If you're struggling in this area, talk with me or one of your teammates at break. If you feel awkward about it, remember transparent accountability is one of the most powerful things we have as followers of Jesus. You will not be elite until you die to the pride of caring about what other people think of you. And let me tell you, I think the pride of caring what other people think about you is one of the most deadly sins in the Church today. This is what causes people to become Pharisees in the 21st century. The more broken and transparent you are, the more powerful you will be when God decides to use you. It's in our weakness He is strong…never forget that. So in conclusion to this lecture, challenge yourself. If you masturbate now and you know it's not pleasing to the Lord because your heart isn't pure in that area, confess your sin to your brothers. Ask for accountability while you reverse the habit of flesh feeding in this area. If you are unsure if you're sinful when you masturbate, I challenge you to sit in God's presence and ask Him if your actions are pleasing in His sight. If you're married, sit down with your wife and talk through this with her. Most importantly, make sure to ask the Spirit to help you walk in Him in every area of life. This life is about pleasing Him alone, and He knows the answer for every weakness we have. He is our help in every time of need. God is so good…"

And He said to me, 'My grace is sufficient for you, for My strength is made perfect in weakness.' Therefore most gladly I will rather boast in my infirmities, that the power of Christ may rest upon me. Therefore I take pleasure in infirmities, in reproaches, in needs, in persecutions, in distresses, for Christ's sake. For when I am weak, then I am strong.
2 Corinthians 12:9-11 (NKJV)

DAILY CHALLENGE

Sit in the Lord's presence and allow Him to examine your heart in regards to this topic. Be courageous enough to ask the Spirit to show you if there's something you need to change or confess in this area. If the Holy Spirit leads, be faithful to confess or respond to what He lays on your heart. Don't let the sun set today without asking the Lord to search your heart on this difficult topic. And if you're married I challenge you to talk to your wife about this very real struggle for men. Remember, there is power in transparent accountability.

Here am I! Send me.

Isaiah 6:8b (NKJV)

During our 20 minute break, the guys and I had a great discussion about our last lecture while knocking out some push-ups since today is our second max push-up challenge. As a Christian man I have never heard this topic discussed head on like this, and I am so grateful it was. I am also so thankful for a group of guys who will be open with each other about such sensitive issues. The atmosphere is one that no one is judging anyone, we are all soldiers on the same team in the same war. It's a pretty remarkable experience, but still difficult nonetheless. Even with this atmosphere some of these lectures are tough because they confront some real personal issues in all of our lives. But I'm ready to continue and learn to live a life of SOULCON. Right before walking back into the classroom we knock out another 25 push-ups as a team just to add to our total for the second push-ups max day of the challenge. My goal is to blow my last max on push-ups day out of the water.

As we all take our seats, Bugsly begins, "Alright gentlemen, I know that last lecture was pretty personal and difficult. I want to remind you all again, this program and challenge is only about growing stronger in Jesus and not yourselves. So if you're thinking any part of this challenge is about bragging rights, you're missing the point. This challenge is only about refinement. This challenge is only about living in the power of the Holy Spirit with your soul and not your flesh. As we really break it down, the little bites we take from the fork that feeds our flesh are the embarrassing ones that no one likes to talk about in public. The bites of food at night when nobody is looking, the judgmental words we tell others, the inappropriate jokes we tell at work, whatever they are, they are things we're not proud of. Areas we need to confess to other soldiers of Jesus, receive prayer for, ask for accountability with, and move on to grow in God's grace for our lives.

I want us all to take a look at the experience Isaiah had with the Lord in Isaiah chapter six. In this chapter Isaiah sees how holy God is, and how unworthy he is. Let me read it to you:

"In the year that King Uzziah died, I saw the Lord sitting on a throne, high and lifted up, and the train of His robe filled the temple. Above it stood seraphim; each one had six wings: with two he covered his face, with two he covered his feet, and with two he flew. And one cried to another and said:

'Holy, holy, holy is the Lord of hosts; The whole earth is full of His glory!'

And the posts of the door were shaken by the voice of him who cried out, and the house was filled with smoke.

So I said: 'Woe is me, for I am undone! Because I am a man of unclean lips, And I dwell in the midst of a people of unclean lips; For my eyes have seen the King, The Lord of hosts.'

Then one of the seraphim flew to me, having in his hand a live coal which he had taken with the tongs from the altar. And he touched my mouth with it, and said: 'Behold, this has touched your lips; Your iniquity is taken away, And your sin purged.'

Also I heard the voice of the Lord, saying: 'Whom shall I send, And who will go for Us?'

Then I said, 'Here am I! Send me.'"

Isaiah 6:1-8 (NKJV)

I pray this is the response we all have to God. I pray after we experience His presence we leave with the same perspective Isaiah had. If we do, we have the key that defeats pride and vanity. That key is humility. That is why during this six-week time you start every day on your knees before the Lord. It's a daily fundamental that will mature you in humility. And when you, like Isaiah, encounter the Lord you will realize how bad you need Jesus and how bad the world around you needs Jesus.

So whether it's gossiping, anger, lustful thoughts, being a workaholic, gluttony, or any other sin; it's imperative we get ourselves in the presence of God's love and mercy. It's imperative that we learn to be holy like God is holy. As men we have to stop justifying our sins and we have to start exposing them to the light of Jesus Christ."

So think clearly and exercise self-control. Look forward to the gracious salvation that will come to you when Jesus Christ is revealed to the world. So you must live as God's obedient children. Don't slip back into your old ways of living to satisfy your own desires. You didn't know any better then. But now you must be holy in everything you do, just as God who chose you is holy. For the Scriptures say, 'You must be holy because I am holy.'

1 Peter 1:13-16 (NLT)

DAILY CHALLENGE

Take 3-5 minutes today and meditate on what you picture Isaiah saw as he was standing looking at God on His throne. Use your imagination to picture all of the details of the room and try to feel what he felt standing there. Make sure there are no distractions, and just set a timer for 3-5 minutes so you can focus all of your attention on the meditation.

Give all your worries and cares to God, for he cares about you. Stay alert! Watch out for your great enemy, the devil. He prowls around like a roaring lion, looking for someone to devour. Stand firm against him, and be strong in your faith. Remember that your Christian brothers and sisters all over the world are going through the same kind of suffering you are.

1 Peter 5:7-9 (NLT)

As I roll over to shut the alarm clock off, I feel such a sense of accomplishment. I broke my last max on push-ups in one twenty-four hour period by 498! I did 1,250 push-ups in one day! I didn't think it would be possible to make an improvement as drastic as that, but I did. As I reflect on yesterday, it's so clear my body is stronger than it has been in my adult life, and maybe ever. But all of the credit goes to the way SOULCON has been teaching us to live in the power of the Holy Spirit and how to train our minds, wills and emotions through this challenge. I can now identify more than ever when my mind is just whining and lying to me. My mind is actually being transformed by the power of the Holy Spirit every day…what an incredible challenge this has been so far! I'm actually looking forward to the 5k team run this morning to help get some of the soreness out of my muscles…and to help prepare me for our test-out on our 5k time next week.

As I get out of bed, I get on my knees to thank God and do what a SOULCON soldier does every morning, and pray the Lord's Prayer out loud for their family and team. Then a cup of black coffee and out to the grinder for the run… I'm actually starting to enjoy this!

As we get to the grinder, we all see Bugsly with a bunch of climbing gear in backpacks for the team.

"Oh no," Tyler says, " what does Bugsly have in store for us today?"

"Good morning gentlemen," Bugsly says with his usual big smirk. "I hope you all slept well! And I hope your chests are all nice and sore from your max day yesterday! If they are, and they should be, it is going to make today even more effective in training your mind to focus. I want each of you to grab a backpack. We're going for a five-mile run this morning with about 20 pounds on our backs. That is the average weight each of you have lost to this point. Some of you have lost more and some less, but we are going to use this morning as a reminder to never go back to where we were physically. At the end of the five-mile run we're going to do a team activity to help us focus our minds on what's truly important. This is one of my favorites at the SOULCON Training Center. So grab your bags, and let's get moving!"

"Embrace the pain, right?" I say to the guys. We all get a laugh as we grab our backpacks and head out for the team run.

We are closing in on the five-mile mark, and we're all shocked at how much weight 20 pounds feels like when you're running. Our run time was much slower than we're used to, but no one stopped to walk, that's a big accomplishment for all of us. I know I was tempted more than once by my mind to walk, but we stayed together and encouraged each other to keep running. Our team is mastering the art of positive self-talk to each other and ourselves. We're also learning how positive peer pressure with brothers in Christ is one of the most powerful things in the world. I cannot thank God enough for the lessons I'm learning here, and just as I think that...I see the high ropes course on the horizon, yikes! As we approach the ropes course they seem to be getting higher off the ground. And one of my fears is heights. Great.

"Great run team! Grab a drink of water and have the breakfast pre-packed in your backpack. While you're eating we will cover the details of the high ropes course.

As you can see, this is not your average high ropes course. This course is 100 feet off the ground. And I don't care who you are; that's high. Your mind will play tricks on you. You're going to feel anxiety come over you, and you're going to feel waves of fear try to enter your mind. This is where we practice what we're learning in the classroom. It is crucial as men that we don't let any negative, fearful or anxious thought stay in our minds. We have to take those thoughts captive to the obedience of Jesus and focus on what

Christ calls us to think on. No matter what external pressures come our way in this life, we have to stay focused and keep our minds full of the fruit of the Spirit. Gentlemen, God cannot do this for us or He would. He gives us freedom to choose what thoughts we dwell on and what thoughts we don't dwell on. So make sure you dwell on positive God filled thoughts during this challenge this morning. And remember if you're struggling to focus your mind, use self-talk. That forces your mind to think whatever it is you're saying. Finish breakfast, then gear up and we'll get going…"

DAILY CHALLENGE

Ask the Lord to show you where you're living in anxiety today. As men we all have worries and anxieties we face and the Lord is waiting to take those cares from us. Once you identify an area where you're worrying or feeling anxious about something, text, call or email someone on your team and ask for prayer with that area. Remember, transparency in your walk with Christ and your SOULCON brothers is key to finishing strong.

Summing it all up, friends, I'd say you'll do best by filling your minds and meditating on things true, noble, reputable, authentic, compelling, gracious—the best, not the worst; the beautiful, not the ugly; things to praise, not things to curse. Put into practice what you learned from me, what you heard and saw and realized. Do that, and God, who makes everything work together, will work you into his most excellent harmonies.
Philippians 4:8-9 (The Message)

We all have our gear on, and it's time to practice training our mind in a challenging environment. I was feeling so confident before right now, I really hope Bugsly doesn't see my knees shaking. For that matter I hope no one on my team does, I can't stop them from rattling.

"Holy Spirit will you please help me face this fear with courage?" I pray quietly. Suddenly a sense of peace enters my heart. I hear the words of Joshua 1:9 in my heart:

"This is my command—be strong and courageous! Do not be afraid or discouraged. For the Lord your God is with you wherever you go."(NLT)

Just then Commander Bugsly calls me over to him, he wants me to start off the activities. Wonderful. As I walk over the guys cheer me on. Bugsly grabs my shoulders, looks me in the eyes and says, "I believe in you, just put into practice what you've learned. Allow the Spirit to control your mind, will and emotions. You can do this."

As he speaks those words of encouragement I feel my courage rise and I look up the ladder. "Thank you sir...I've got this!" I grab the ladder and take my first step up to conquer one of my fears. There's no turning back now...the whole team is watching.

Step by step up the ladder I keep reminding myself that God is with me. And I make sure I keep my eyes fixed on the pole where the steps of the ladder are. I know looking down might bring fear into my mind. As I reach the top of the ladder, which is just an extremely high telephone pole with pegs that make up the ladder on it. I feel the pole swaying in the wind. I am officially out of the covering of the trees, there is nothing to block the wind. I reach up and grab the tiny wooden platform that looks like it will barely hold my weight. I slowly step up on the platform and look across to the other platform, that's a long way. There are two ropes, one for your feet and one for your hands to hold on to. I can hear my team cheering me on, but honestly they are so far down there it's hard to make out their words.

I feel fear flood my body as the wind picks up, and my knees start shaking uncontrollably again. It's just me and my thoughts up here and the negative thoughts are winning. So I start to think about the verse in 1 Peter 5:7 about worry and how Bugsly constantly teaches the class the importance of a worry free mind. So I identify this toxic thinking, and eliminate it by enforcing positive self-talk. I start speaking personalized scriptures to myself from Philippians 4:13 and Joshua 1:9, "I can do all things through Christ who strengthens me. I am strong and courageous, I will not be terrified and I will not be dismayed. I will trust that God is with me everywhere I go." I just keep repeating it and peace starts to enter my mind. But the fear isn't gone. I have to take this step onto this rope in the face of my fear. So I start speaking louder, and I walk over to the ropes. I can vaguely hear the guys cheering me on below. So with looking only at the ropes, making sure I don't look down, I do it. I take my first step on this tiny little rope, making sure my hands have a tight grip on the rope. I take this journey step by step and I am committed to never stop speaking God's Word out loud to myself. I continually feel fear trying to overtake my mind and control my body, but the self-talk is helping me stay in control of my mind so I can focus on the next step. Before I know it, my next step is onto the other platform! I made it! Praise God!

Now it's time for the victory jump. The victory jump is where you jump off the platform and you let the belayer, Commander Bugsly bring you down. This is the only way down. With a heart full of confidence, I look straight up in the sky, still committed to not looking down, and I jump off the platform 100 feet off the ground.

My stomach feels like it is going to rush up out of my mouth and then I feel the rope catch…I made it, just an easy ride to the ground from here!

When I get to the ground I am surrounded with high fives from the team and a sense of pride in the Lord. I did it… I learned how to overcome fear. God is so good…

DAILY CHALLENGE

Find three verses to personalize, and start using them for your positive self-talk. Put this fundamental of mental toughness as an elite soldier of Christ into practice at least three times today. Don't just say these verses with the voice in your mind, speak the scriptures out-loud. Commit to making self-talk with scriptures a daily habit in your life.

DAY 33
SAVORING THE VICTORIES

Far better is it to dare mighty things, to win glorious triumphs, even though checkered by failure... than to rank with those poor spirits who neither enjoy nor suffer much, because they live in a gray twilight that knows not victory nor defeat.

Theodore Roosevelt

Walking into the classroom this morning, today is the second max squat day of the challenge, I look over to Alfred and hold my coffee up for a "cheers." At that point I feel the soreness from the max push-up day and laugh, then I notice the soreness in my abs from our max sit-up day. Alfred and I get a good laugh with how our legs might feel tomorrow after our max squat day. But we both praise God for what He has done to this point in our lives at SOULCON.

"We're making it brother!" I say to Alfred.

"Making it? We're thriving! All of this soreness and all! This experience with our team has transformed my perspective as a man of God on this earth. I have always had a warrior on the inside of me, I just didn't know how to let that warrior out. And during my daughter's fight with cancer, and then her death, the warrior in me was buried by the food I would cover it with. But I am learning, with you all pushing me that living as a warrior is yielding to the power of the Spirit daily. That is where the battle is...and I will fight it everyday. Thank you for pushing and encouraging me brother!"

"My pleasure and honor, love you man!" I say back to Alfred as I give him a big hug. "I'm excited to see what Commander Bugsly has for us today!"

"Good morning gentlemen!" Bugsly says, "I hope you're all having a great start to the second max squat day! Today, I have my friend here to share with us from his journey on a reality TV show as well as from when he served with me in special forces. This is a guy who lost over 200 pounds over a year, faced his flesh head on, and has a heart bigger than any man I know. Please give him a warm

SOULCON welcome."

"Thank you all so much! I count it an honor to be with y'all. I hope what I have to share with you will minister to you as much as it did to me when I learned it. Like Commander Bugsly said, I was on a national television show for weight-loss. It was, to say the least, life changing. At this point, I was already a Christian, but I had no control of my soul. I would wake up every morning living in the control of the desires of my flesh especially with food. The fork that fed my mouth was a weapon the enemy was using to slowly kill me off. I just couldn't resist the temptation the fork brought to my life with food. Food became my closest friend and my comfort. I was hiding a lot of emotions with every bite I would take. From the time I woke up to the time I went to bed, I was feeding the appetites of my flesh, knowing I was out of control.

One day, my wife encouraged me to go try-out for this TV show. My wife has always been an incredible pillar in my life, spiritually and emotionally. So I humbly listened to her. I went to the show and felt shame and embarrassment, but I was honest in every interview about where I was in life. And that was so difficult...

About a week later I got a phone call that I was selected to be on this show. A sudden flood of every bad emotion you could think of flooded my mind and heart. I just wanted to lock myself in a closet and eat. But I just knew in my heart this was a door God was opening...I knew on the other side of this door was a battle with the flesh I had been feeding bite by bite with my fork for the last ten years. I accepted, and left my wife and two kids to go onto the show.

When I got to the location of the show, it was like I was back in military boot camp. Like Commander Bugsly said, I served with him as one of the world's elite soldiers. I lived and breathed excellence, and I was committed to being the best I could in every area. But one deployment changed all of that. Our team got ambushed, we suffered serious injury, and I lost my best friend in that ambush. His death was a sledgehammer to my heart...you see, I made it out physically, but I didn't make it out mentally or emotionally. I just couldn't face another deployment, another possibility of losing one of my brothers. I eventually quit special forces, and I felt like I quit everything else. I spent the next ten years finding comfort in food and my family paid a hard price for that.

When I stepped on the gym floor of that reality TV show, all of those military emotions came back. I felt like I was going to hyperventilate. We hadn't even gotten situated and they wanted us to start our first workout...we hadn't even had our first meal. And that was shocking to me, and horrifying. Eating was where I found comfort.

I will never forget the next event, and that's what I pray you all take away from my story. After about an hour and a half into our first workout I broke down crying. Completely embarrassed. Then one of the trainers came up to me and what he said changed my life.

This trainer said, 'No matter what you have done or where you've been in your life, your survival depends on you making the choice to live in the present. Your survival is dependent on you celebrating the small victories, allowing failure to fuel your drive for success, and never allow giving up to be something you accept.'

Just those few words sparked something within me I hadn't seen since I served with Commander Bugsly. This was the moment I asked God, for the first time, to help me break free from this addiction, to help me forgive myself for my friend's death on the battlefield. Peace finally filled my heart. I was confident God healed my emotional heart. But I knew my physical heart, my brain and my muscular skeletal system had to catch up to that healing. I had done a lot of damage to all of those things over the last ten years, and I knew I had some work to do. So with the help of the trainer and that show, I lost 200 pounds in one year.

To this point I have lost over 250 pounds and I am now living at my optimal weight and health. I have learned to live with my mind, will and emotions controlled by the Spirit in every area...and not the fork that feeds my flesh. After the show I got a message from Bugsly and we reconnected. He shared with me where he was and what the SOULCON Training Center was about. I fell in love with this challenge course. I start my day, every day, with the Lord's Prayer on my knees, and I am committed to living a SOULCON lifestyle. So know when I pray, I am praying for you all, my SOULCON brothers of war. When you choose to find your identity in the cross instead of the fork, know I am with you. I pray my life and this challenge inspires you to live with this focus for the rest of your mission on this earth. Please never forget what you're learning here. Keep up the great work and thank you for your time!"

Bugsly stands up and says, "Class, please join me in thanking my brother, my fellow soldier, and a warrior of Christ for sharing with us today!"

DAILY CHALLENGE

Share one motivational quote from this journey with someone in your life. It can be with a text, email or social media message. We always have to remember everyone is fighting a battle in this life and one encouraging word or quote can change the course of someone's day. Be the Light.

The Lord is a warrior; Yahweh is His name!

Exodus 15:3 NLT

As our class breaks from the first lecture of the day, Commander Bugsly hands us all a sheet of paper. It's a picture of the different pieces of God's armor in Ephesians chapter six.

"We'll cover this when we come back in from break" Commander Bugsly says as our class is going out to knock out some squats and grab a cup of coffee.

"Wow... What an incredible story that guy has!" Alfred says to me as we're walking down the hall. "No kidding. I couldn't imagine how hard that was for him to go through those challenges on national television. What a warrior."

As we're grabbing a cup of coffee we knock out a set of 50 squats. Again, we are working to beat our previous record with squats. There are some guys in the class with knees that aren't as healthy as others so they don't go as low. But everyone is doing what they can with what they have. As long as we are challenging ourselves, we're on the right path. As for me, I am thankful my knees are healthy, so I can go down pretty low with my squats. I am not sure I will be that thankful about that tomorrow. But here's to embracing the pain.

As our break winds down, we head back into the classroom and grab a seat. I grab the paper on my desk and look at the different pieces of armor from Ephesians chapter six. I read through the text, and on the bottom of the page in big bold letters it says:

Elite Soldiers Know Their Need For Armor. Don't Leave Home Without It.

"Alright gentlemen, let's dive into our next topic, God's armor. This is something you typically see in Sunday schools, with a cute little warrior all decked out and ready to go play on the play ground with his friends. It is crucial to your lives that you don't view this armor in this way. This armor is crucial to the success of your lives, the success of you finishing strong in Christ, and the success of you advancing the Light into the darkness.

I want to clarify one thing, this is not King David's armor, this is not Joshua's armor, and this is not Samson's armor. Some days I wish God would have given us armor like theirs! There are some people that just need some Old Testament love. But Christ has called us to a new way of thinking and fighting. Gentlemen, as bad as we want it at times, our battle is not physical. It's not swords and shields we can hold and use in the physical, it's an invisible war we fight now.

When I was about to deploy in the military, I knew my special forces team and I were going somewhere the "normal" forces couldn't go, or weren't trained to go. I knew we were going into the dark areas of the world where the enemy was looking to kill us. So during our briefings our team would listen, take notes of the enemy activity and how they would attack, and we would make sure we would grab the appropriate weapons from the armory for the warfare we were going to engage in.

We never had a person on our team forget their weapons or act like they could accomplish the mission with their bare hands and no ammo. We knew to accomplish the mission we needed the right weapons. I say this because most of us overlook Ephesians chapter six. I call this God's armory. Before I leave my house every morning I visualize myself putting each piece on. I stop by the armory, recognize my need for these weapons, and head into this world ready for battle. I want to encourage you guys to do the same thing. Please do not leave your weapons on the shelf collecting dust.

As you guys are preparing your minds to live as elite soldiers for Jesus Christ every morning, please, never go into a day without putting your armor on. This armor will make you effective and save your lives. And we only have access to this armor because of what Jesus did on the cross. Jesus died and was resurrected so we could live eternal, with no fear of death, and fight with His armor to advance His Kingdom on this earth. I want you to mediate on this throughout the remainder of your squat day, and use your imagination to see these weapons and learn to love them."

A final word: Be strong in the Lord and in his mighty power. Put on all of God's armor so that you will be able to stand firm against all strategies of the devil. For we are not fighting against flesh-and-blood enemies, but against evil rulers and authorities of the unseen world, against mighty powers in this dark world, and against evil spirits in the heavenly places.

Therefore, put on every piece of God's armor so you will be able to resist the enemy in the time of evil. Then after the battle you will still be standing firm. Stand your ground, putting on the belt of truth and the body armor of God's righteousness. For shoes, put on the peace that comes from the Good News so that you will be fully prepared. In addition to all of these, hold up the shield of faith to stop the fiery arrows of the devil. Put on salvation as your helmet, and take the sword of the Spirit, which is the word of God.

Pray in the Spirit at all times and on every occasion. Stay alert and be persistent in your prayers for all believers everywhere.
Ephesians 6:10-18 (NLT)

DAILY CHALLENGE

Read over these verses and use your imagination to see and feel this armor on you. See yourself as the soldier God created you to be and commit to never leave home without this armor.

'Bring all the tithes into the storehouse so there will be enough food in my Temple. If you do,' says the Lord of Heaven's Armies, 'I will open the windows of heaven for you. I will pour out a blessing so great you won't have enough room to take it in! Try it! Put me to the test! Your crops will be abundant, for I will guard them from insects and disease. Your grapes will not fall from the vine before they are ripe,' says the Lord of Heaven's Armies. 'Then all nations will call you blessed, for your land will be such a delight,' says the Lord of Heaven's Armies.

Malachi 3:10-12 (NLT)

As our team grabs donuts and coffee, we praise God for sweet food and we all head into the chapel for our last worship service here at SOULCON. My heart is filled with thanksgiving for what God has done during this time. I finally feel like I have the strength to submit control of my soul to the Spirit to be satisfied instead of finding comfort from the fork that feeds my flesh. And it's a great feeling to know I can have a few donuts, as a reward for my hard work, and then have the ability to stop whenever I want with the sweet food. Praise God! This is a major victory for me in my walk with the Spirit.

As I walk into the worship center, I sit down to focus on and enjoy my donuts and coffee. And the crazy thing is that I'm actually starting to enjoy the black coffee…pretty cool! I lean over and talk to the guys about how thankful I am that max week is over.

"That was brutal! I'm excited to see our test-out times this next week, and share those results and this experience with our families on graduation day." It will have been six weeks since we've seen our families, and I know I can speak for all of us when I say we're thrilled to see them! We all feel like new men, men on fire to carry our cross and follow Jesus. I'm really growing in a love for these guys and I'm so thankful for the brotherhood we are developing.

After having some time to eat and fellowship, the worship band comes out and the service begins. Typically, I'm the one who tunes out during worship time, but with everything I've learned about Jesus over this challenge, I cannot help but find joy in giving Him praise.

With each song my heart overflows with thankfulness for what this challenge has done to this point in my life. One day, I will be with these brothers sitting with Jesus in Heaven, the fight of faith will be over, and we will feast eternally with my brothers and sisters in Christ. But until then, times like these encourage me to focus on living the life of an elite solider for Jesus. With purpose in each step, clothed in His power daily, and not conforming to the pattern of this world.

After the worship the SOULCON Chaplin stands up and brings a message about living to give. I'm always excited for what this guy has to bring us...

"Good morning gentlemen! I hope you're all having a great Sabbath and second feast day! I know this challenge is a difficult one, but some of the lessons you will have learned during this six weeks will impact the rest of your life if you allow them to. Learning to submit your mind, will and emotions to the Holy Spirit every morning is the single most important thing we can do as followers of Jesus. We always have to remember that anything we do in the Spirit is eternal and anything we do in the flesh is temporary. So live for the eternal in every area.

Today I want to cover finances, and committing the rest of your time on earth to steward your finances with excellence to your Commander in Chief, Jesus. You see, every good thing you have, He has given you, and God desires for all of you to be wise stewards with the lot He has entrusted you, this includes your money. As a SOULCON soldier of Jesus Christ, we are proactive with the Gospel, we are movers and shakers and we will look for opportunities to be used by God in every area. In my opinion tithes and offerings are one of the most overlooked areas in the church today. Gentlemen, we cannot let this happen. Throughout scripture God shows us the importance of giving our money back to Him and the work of the Church. Please turn with me to 1 Timothy 6:10 and I will read this out of the New Living Translation:

'For the love of money is the root of all kinds of evil. And some people, craving money, have wandered from the true faith and pierced themselves with many sorrows.'

This SOULCON challenge is focused on learning to find satisfaction in the Spirit and not the sinful desires of our flesh, and this is a crucial area to consider in the life of a bondservant of Jesus Christ. We have to make sure we act on our faith every day, because without action our faith is dead.

'Isn't it obvious that God-talk without God-acts is outrageous nonsense?' James 2:20 (The Message)

We have to be men of God with our actions speaking louder than our words. It's easy to talk like a Christian, but living as a Christian is learning the joy in dying to our sinful desires. And money is an area we have to learn the joy of dying in. The love of money is enticing, it's something that promises so much more than it brings, and as men, loving our money and success more than God is an easy sin to justify and hide. But know one thing men, we can fool other people, but God sees every time we ignore His whispers inside of us.

'Do not be deceived, God is not mocked; for whatever a man sows, that he will also reap.' Galatians 6:7 (NKJV)

So commit to sowing seeds to the Spirit with your finances every time you have the chance. Don't let one opportunity pass where you can sow seeds to God's work and Kingdom on this earth. No other investment on this earth pays a higher reward. Not only is the handling of our money the only place in scripture where God says to test Him, it's also the only place where you find the love of an item, known as the root of all evil. We have to constantly practice making our money serve God so we don't end up serving our money.

Keep up the great work SOULCON soldiers, and please, commit this day to never let an opportunity pass to sow into God's Kingdom. Commit today to lead in this area in your home church. One practice I have, and I challenge you with is to never let an offering time or plate pass without putting something into it. No matter the dollar amount, it's a practice I use that I challenge you to make a lifestyle of practicing keeping God the main love of your heart. Here's to leaving it all on the field for Jesus."

As the service concludes, I think how I have never viewed tithing as something we should be excited about until now. It's always been something I've considered as an option in my life, and something that they only did in the Old Testament. But Chaplain helped everyone learn the importance of adding works to our faith in every area of our lives, and challenged our class to do our best to never let a tithe and offering plate go by without giving our best. That's a challenge, like many here at SOULCON I commit to making a lifestyle.

DAILY CHALLENGE

Your challenge today is to commit to giving God your best with finances. This, like any decision we make starts with a decision to obey Jesus in our mind and heart. The Holy Spirit won't force us to obey Him, but He longs for us to live in joyful obedience to Him… even with our finances. So commit to never letting a week go by without giving God at least 10% of your income. Lead by example in your home and church in this area. Pray about taking the offering plate challenge as well.

WEEK 05 RESULTS

Be sure to share your results and encourage others
going through the challenge on the SOULCON App.

WEEK 05 REFLECTIONS

Be sure to share your reflections and encourage others going through the challenge on the SOULCON App.

THE SOULCON CHALLENGE OBJECTIVES:

- Pray the Lord's Prayer out loud, on your knees – EVERY DAY
- No carbs after 3pm from grains and breads (sweet potatoes, vegetables, and berries are the only carbs you can have).
  - Track your caloric intake in the book or on an app, just record everything except for your three feast days.
- Drink at least 64oz of water a day
- Exercise at least 30 minutes 5 days a week
  - Run, walk or crawl, two 5ks (3.1 miles) a week
- Before you leave home for the day do 40 push-ups (or as many as you can)
- Sleep 6-8 hours a night (excluding feast days)
- Evangelism: Hand out a total of ten Gospel tracts to people you don't know.

For God has not given us a spirit of fear and timidity, but of power, love, and self-discipline.

2 Timothy 1:7 (NLT)

This morning I hear the alarm clock go off, and I feel like I have a carbohydrate hangover. It's shocking how badly I feel the morning after a feast day. I guess input really does equal output. It just blows my mind that I used to eat like that all of the time. Part of the training here is the psychological component of feasting and how important it is to take a break from healthy eating and exercise to rest. Even Bugsly teaches us the morning after a feast day is the most crucial day of the healthy week. He reminds us that is when we can practice overcoming the desire to allow our body to dictate our performance in life. I am starting to understand that more. All I feel like doing is laying in bed, but I need to force this body to get out of my comfort zone, spend time with Jesus and then head out for our last team 5k before our test-out on Thursday. As I roll out of bed and get on my knees, I start praying the Lord's Prayer and thanksgiving fills my heart. I have never had discipline like this in my life, I just thought if I was supposed to be healthy the Holy Spirit would do a supernatural work in my life. I am learning that the cross was the supernatural work, and when we embrace the death of our lives and comfort in this world, then we find true life in Jesus. I count it as an honor to pick up my cross daily now. Wow... God is so good.

As I run up to the grinder, there are backpacks on the ground once again. I look to Tyler and shake my head.

"What's Bugsly have up his sleeve today?" Tyler says.

Alfred chimes in, "I'm not sure, but those backpacks look like they were made for airplanes and not hiking."

"Good morning gents!" Bugsly yells as he comes running up to the team. "I hope you're all ready for a great day! This is our last week together and I promise it's one of the best ones yet! Everyone grab a backpack and let's get moving. We have an exciting day today!"

As I grab my bag, a chill runs down my spine. Crap, it's a parachute. I have never been skydiving, and I honestly have no desire, at all, I mean I have been afraid of heights my whole life. But Christ helped me though the high ropes course and I am committed to learning and finishing everything this challenge has to offer. So I strap on my bag and join my team on the run. Facing my fear head on.

After a little over four miles of jogging, which is one more mile than we were ready for, especially after the carbohydrate hangover I woke up with, we see a plane on the horizon. Chills run over my body.

"I am sure you've figured it out by now," Commander Bugsly says, "We are going skydiving today! To this point we have learned to live by submitting our souls to the Spirit everyday, but we're focusing on eliminating fear from our lives today.

No matter who you are, there should be a little fear crossing through your mind when you think about jumping out of an airplane. We are going to learn how to apply 2 Timothy 1:7 in our daily lives by applying it to our minds and hearts before we jump out of this plane today. So let's get the training knocked out so we can get above 10,000 feet!"

Walking into the solo jump-training center, the thought goes through my head that I might not live to see my family this weekend at graduation. Just as that thought runs through my mind, Alfred pats me on the shoulder and encourages me with a timely scripture.

"Don't let fear get in brother, remember the scripture we said was one of our favorites at the team cookout last night,

'For to me, living means living for Christ, and dying is even better.' Philippians 1:21 (NLT)

So let's enjoy this. I mean, we ran a 10 mile run together, surely that was more likely to kill us than this!"

Alfred has been through so much, but he still encourages the team constantly and has a great sense of humor.

"Thank you brother," I say back to him, "let's do this!"

DAILY CHALLENGE

Take time to reflect on your feast day. How did you do? Did you stay under the control of the Spirit or did you lose control and fall into gluttony? Either way, write down a few key points about having a successful day off from healthy eating. If you fell into gluttony, repent and write down tips for yourself on how to have a successful feast day next time. If you did great, write a few tips that helped you walk in the Spirit with the enjoyment of food. Remember, life with Christ is all about walking in His strength and power and not our own.

This is my command—be strong and courageous! Do not be afraid or discouraged. For the Lord your God is with you wherever you go.

Joshua 1:9 (NLT)

The training is complete. It's time to board the plane with the guys. I made the decision to pass on eating lunch just in case my nerves get the best of me. While boarding the plane, Commander Bugsly shares Joshua 1:9 with us and tells the team about the importance of trusting God's Word more than our emotions. I absolutely love how direct Bugsly is with the Word of God, he doesn't hold back at all, and he delivers it to our team like the special forces commander he is.

As we walk toward the plane, I become more and more thankful I made the decision to pass on lunch. My stomach feels like it's going to toss the cookies I ate at our team cookout last night. But in the face of our fears, everyone boards the plane and sits down. We have our gear on and we're ready to go.

The plane starts down the runway, and I know we are all at the point of no return. I look over at Tyler and he has a grin the size of Texas on his face. I can't remember that guy ever showing fear. But he looks over at me and nods. I nod back and feel a sense of brotherly courage come over me. We're in this together, just like we have been in the other challenges of life together back home. I love that guy…

About 15 minutes later, our plane crosses over 10,000 feet and gets to the jump-zone. Commander Bugsly stands up, smiles, and opens the jump door. I take a big breath and recite Joshua 1:9 quietly to myself. I think of the value of learning to overcome my fears, learning to truly live and learning to trust God fully with my life. This is extremely difficult but priceless.

Bugsly calls the team over. We're all standing by the door and he starts sending the team out one by one. I slowly slip to the back, but before I know it, Commander and I are the only ones left to jump. He looks at me, reaches his hand out and says, "Let's do this together!" I smile back, with as much courage as I can muster in the moment, and nod as I grab his hand.

"On three!" he yells, "One… Two… Three!"

At that moment we both step out of the plane. I feel the rush of the wind and I look behind us to see our plane flying away. Wow! I did it! And it feels incredible! I look over at Bugsly with an actual smile this time, and I nod in gratitude with tears in my eyes. I'm not sure if it's from the wind blowing or from the emotion, but there are tears. He nods back and reaches his fist out for a fist bump. I reach out and bump his fist back, feeling like a fearless warrior.

As we're both free falling to the earth, the excitement of being a follower of Christ fills my mind. I survey the earth, how beautiful it looks, and think how big and majestic God is. Right here in the air, falling to the earth, I repent for ever fearing and I repent for not viewing God with the fear and awe He is worthy of. Falling to the earth I commit to be a fearless disciple of Jesus for the rest of my life.

I look over and check our altitude and see 4,000 feet. I reach back, praying my chute was packed right, and pull the chord to deploy my parachute. The chute deploys great and everything slows down. Time to sit back and just make sure I nail the landing. We had extensive training, so I feel very confident with this.

As the ground approaches, I do what we were trained to do, and I nail the landing. The guys run over greeting the Commander and me with high fives and bear hugs. I did it! I overcame my fear, I feel like a new, fearless man of God.

Commander Bugsly gathers the team for a prayer and a word of encouragement, "Brothers, well done! We did it! I am so proud of you all! I want to encourage you to never forget this moment. Never forget the rush of overcoming fear, the rush of living fearlessly on this earth, or in this case over this earth, and never forget the rush of trusting Jesus wholly with your lives."

We all regroup and head back to the training center without the packs, praise God, and without the heavy weight of the fear and anxiety most of us had running over here.

DAILY CHALLENGE

Think about your life with Jesus. What are some areas of your life you feel fear? Is it public speaking? Maybe it's with talking to a stranger about your personal relationship with Jesus. Ask the Spirit to reveal to you where fear has been holding you back from living in the fullness of God's power. Once the Spirit reveals this to you, commit to living fearless in this area. Work on trusting God more than your emotions.

The scroll of Isaiah the prophet was handed to him. He unrolled the scroll and found the place where this was written: 'The Spirit of the Lord is upon me, for he has anointed me to bring Good News to the poor. He has sent me to proclaim that captives will be released, that the blind will see, that the oppressed will be set free, and that the time of the Lord's favor has come.' He rolled up the scroll, handed it back to the attendant, and sat down. All eyes in the synagogue looked at him intently.

Luke 4:17-20 (NLT)

Today I feel like a new man as I walk into the class for Commander Bugsly's final lecture. I think about how much I'm going to miss his teaching, his leadership and this environment with my brothers of SOULCON.

As I sit down, I'm ready to be pushed and grow more in my relationship with Christ. I quietly pray and ask God to always keep my heart and mind in place like this, clothed in His Spirit and in a place of vigilance to advance the Kingdom by force like an elite soldier.

"Good morning brothers! I feel at this point calling you brothers is more fitting with the experiences we have developed over the past six weeks. You have been through the challenges of this program, and you have excelled in them all. I have the utmost confidence that you will all beat your original 5k time, your push-up and sit-up numbers. I am excited to soon call you true SOULCON brothers of Christ. Graduation is so close, let's keep up the great work and finish strong.

Today there is one thing that I want to make sure I clear up before we continue on and finish this challenge. This is an extremely controversial issue in the Body of Christ and one that has done a lot of damage to the advancement of the Good News of Jesus Christ. We're going to cover free will and predestination. So get that mind ready, prepare your heart, and let's do this. I know this is a tough subject but let's face it head on.

I want to share with you a mission I was assigned by this country, and one God used years later to clear up this challenging issue in my own personal life.

About 15 years ago, the special forces team I was assigned to got called in on a weekend. Everyone seemed excited as we headed to the briefing room. As we all walked in and sat down, our Commander shut the door. He put images on the screen of the mission and the mission objective. Our team felt a wave of excitement come over us. We had found someone who had been missing in action (MIA) for three years. This person was officially considered lost by our country. Our intel team had found this person, who had been taken captive as a prisoner of war (POW) by the enemy without us knowing about it and our assignment was to carryout the mission given to us by our Commander to set this captive free.

Our team did just that; we carried out the mission to the letter. We saved the life of a person who was being held captive by the enemy and who, until we found out about this soldier, was considered lost by this country. We all risked our lives for this one person. And I know I can speak for everyone on my team when I say, we would all do it again.

Our team saved that person's life, because we knew our mission and we obeyed our orders. We didn't sit around and argue the point saying maybe this person was predestined to be lost by the country and there was nothing we could do about it so we shouldn't even go. And we didn't debate on how that person could just free himself if he truly wanted to be free. There are no theological obstacles on special forces teams, you either obey your mission objectives given to you by your commander or you get off the team. In this mission and every mission I was apart of in combat zones our team didn't delay, we accomplished the mission assigned to us because we followed the plan we were assigned. We obeyed first and asked questions and voiced our opinions later.

I tell you this story to illustrate the mission you have as soldiers of Jesus Christ. Our clear-cut mission is to trust and obey Jesus as the Lord of our lives. Our two top mission objectives are to love God fully and love our neighbors as ourselves. Praise God these things are simple, and it's imperative we come to the conclusion there are things as bondservants of the Almighty God that we will never fully understand, and that's okay. Predestination and free will are areas God has intentionally not fully disclosed to us, so we cannot let them slow us down in our advancement of the Good News. No matter what we determine is the truth on this topic, it is crucial that we keep our focus on the mission given to us by our Commander in Chief. Let's obey the mission first and ask questions on this topic behind closed doors with other mature men and women of God and voice our opinions there, but do not let it slow down your main mission objective with evangelism. Do not leave your mission up to someone else to carryout.

Go into all the world and preach the Good News to everyone.
Mark 16:15b (NLT)

If we don't obey this order given to us by Jesus, people will suffer in the captivity of the enemy on this earth and possibly in Hell for eternity. Saving people is God's business, but obeying God to share the Good News is ours. We are soldiers in His army, He gives orders and we obey, period. The results are in His hands and He is smarter than all of us, so let's not try to figure out every move God makes. Someday we can ask Him everything and we will have the mental capacity to understand it, for now, let's just commit to obey His Word and trust Him with the outcome.

So please commit with me, from this day forward that you will trust and obey God more than your own personal theology. The truth is there are hurting people out there that need you to share the unconditional love of Jesus Christ with them, and that message has the power to set the captives free. Let's live the great commission everyday, let's live to honor and obey our Commander in Chief.

DAILY CHALLENGE

Text one of the guys on your team and ask him what he thought about today's devotional. Remember it's in accountability we grow stronger in the Spirit, so commit to talking through the tough subjects with each other. If you disagree with each other, that's okay. Just make sure nothing comes between you and your obedience to God's Word.

Winning is not a sometime thing; it's an all time thing. You don't win once in a while, you don't do things right once in a while, you do them right all the time. Winning is habit. Unfortunately, so is losing.

Vince Lombardi

Well, today is the day. Today is the day we all find out how much all of our training has paid off. I understand that this test-out isn't just physical; this is a mental and emotional learning and developing experience. As a three part being (body, soul and spirit), I now know everything that I do is a combination of all three. So I'm exited to see the improvements I've made over the last six-weeks in my body, soul and spirit with this test.

As our team meets together on the grinder to get ready to start our test-out, Commander Bugsly walks up and says, "Good morning brothers! I hope you're ready to push yourself to your new limits today! I count it an honor to be your instructor, and I love how much you have all grown in who you are in Christ.

I just want to remind everyone to remember what you've learned. From the ice bath training, to understanding who you are in Christ, this is a place to practice in the art of winning in Christ with your mind and emotions. As you have learned, your body is stronger than you know; it's your mind and emotions that need training. So focus on this scripture when your mind and emotions start to tell you to stop pushing your body today:

'Don't you realize that in a race everyone runs, but only one person gets the prize? So run to win! All athletes are disciplined in their training. They do it to win a prize that will fade away, but we do it for an eternal prize. So I run with purpose in every step. I am not just shadowboxing. I discipline my body like an athlete, training it to do what it should. Otherwise, I fear that after preaching to others I myself might be disqualified.' 1 Corinthians 9:24-27 (NLT)

As your body gets tired, focus on the athletes who train solely for a medal in the Olympics. They commit their lives for one event. We are putting our bodies through this pain so we can be the most effective soldiers of Jesus possible. That's something to suffer well for. Don't just survive this test-out, focus on winning. Hear the voice of your flesh scream, and overcome by positive self-talk, meditation and any other mind control trick you've learned. Let's get started!"

Feeling motivated, I get down in the push-up position, and we begin. I start cranking out the push-ups and I feel great. No flesh screaming yet! As I pass my previous test-in number I start to feel a little fatigue set in. My mind is starting to tell me to stop, but I keep on pushing. I'm now 25 push-ups past my test-in number and my body is shaking. All I can think of is how bad I want to discipline my body for Jesus by walking in His strength. So I push out 10 more before I fall to the ground. I did it! I crushed my test-in number and I'm so proud of how I overcame the feeling to quit from my flesh.

As we move on to sit-ups, I go through the same emotions, but through prayer I overcome the emotions and temptations to quit early and I crush my test-in number with sit-ups too! Now on to the run...

Starting out on the run, it takes me a while to catch my stride, and then I feel everything line up. I feel, for the first time in my life, like I'm actually a runner. I can tell my pace is faster than it has been before but it seems almost effortless, so I speed up. I'm excited to hear my flesh scream so I can practice winning in Christ.

Almost finished, I turn the corner and see the finish line about a half-mile ahead. My breathing is now out of control, I've pushed a little too hard. Everything in me is telling me to slow down, but I start yelling back and putting self-talk into practice. I start yelling, "I'm a strong finisher in Christ. I am strong, courageous, and in Christ I am a winner. Don't quit now, finish strong. Embrace the pain!" These words seem to calm the screams of my mind, and pump up my adrenaline... it's working! So I push a little harder. As I cross the finish line I see that I beat my previous time by two minutes and thirty seconds. Wow! Praise God! I did it! I might throw up, but I did it! It was worth all of the pain. I learned the joy in overcoming the flesh with physical fitness so I can practice staying on the course

Christ has for me. This SOULCON stuff has completely transformed my view of who I am in Christ...

DAILY CHALLENGE

Share your test-out time with your team with a group text or email. Let them know how you did and what areas of the SOULCON journey helped you the most in pushing yourself to your new limits.

Concentrate all your thoughts upon the work at hand. The sun's rays do not burn until brought to a focus.

Alexander Graham Bell

Rolling out of bed, I hit my knees and pray the Lord's Prayer. As I do I feel a sense of awe come over me for all God has done and for everything He is. Even though I have been away from my family and I've pushed myself harder than I have in my life, I am so grateful for the man the Holy Spirit has transformed me into during this time. I know my mind, will, and emotions will never be the same after this experience.

After spending time with Jesus in prayer and devotion, I grab a cup of coffee and head out to the grinder with my team. The physical challenges are behind us, but we've all learned no one here at the SOULCON Training Center wastes any time. So we're ready for another incredible day.

As I walk up to the grinder, sipping my coffee, I see Commander Bugsly with an AR-15 strapped on his back and a big grin on his face. I look over and see 12 rifles laid out on the grass next to the grinder. Excitement floods my body because I absolutely love shooting.

"Good morning brothers!" Bugsly says, "I want to congratulate all of you on beating your test-in scores yesterday! You have all done great throughout this challenge with learning the importance of being controlled by the Holy Spirit in every area of your lives. As you know, yesterday was our last physical test here at SOULCON, but as an elite soldier of Jesus Christ our training is never finished. Our goal is to continue to pick up our cross daily and allow His Spirit to help us make our mind and emotions look like Jesus more every day until we're with Him in Heaven. The will to be committed to this type of excellence in every area of life with Jesus is the heart of this program. We are going to head over to the shooting range. But unlike most trips to the shooting range, this one is going to be a little different. So grab your rifle and let's get moving."

I look over at Tyler and smile. The thrill of running with a rifle on our backs is something I thought I would never experience. As we all strap them on our backs, I give a few of the guys high fives, and we start out for a run to the shooting range.

As we approach the range we realized our team ran our fastest pace yet. It was probably the feeling of being a warrior with the rifle on our backs, or that our final destination was shooting these sweet AR-15s on the range, either way, we killed that run. What a blast…

Bugsly sets his rifle down on the range and speaks up, "Alright team, set your rifles on the range and grab a piece of fruit and a protein bar. We'll be out here for a few hours so make sure you get your energy in. As you eat, I'll brief you on what we're going to do this morning and give you some time for your food to digest. You'll need it."

"Wait, what?! Why will we need to let our food digest?! Man…I wonder what Bugsly is planning?" I say quietly to Alfred with some frustration in my voice.

"Today we're going to focus on the importance of calming your mind and your heart to focus on hitting the target. This is more than just learning to shoot; this is learning to eliminate the distractions in your mind and emotions as disciples of Jesus to make sure you hit the 'targets' the Lord places in front of you.

During my time with special forces groups I served on a few deployments as a sniper. There was extensive training to be able to be used as a sniper by this country, but the main thing I learned was allowing distraction to settle into my mind and emotions was detrimental to my mission. If I allowed my mind to become anxious about the possibility of getting noticed, or the chance of missing the target and my team becoming exposed, or allowed my heart-rate to climb due to the external pressures on my body, more than likely I would not accomplish the mission I was assigned to.

So as you grab your rifle today I want you to focus on calming your mind, keeping your heart-rate low, and keeping your focus on hitting the target. Don't even think about the kick of the rifle, just breath in normal and as you're breathing out slowly keep your eyes on the target, slowly pull the trigger until it goes off. Just keep your eyes on the target. Let the shot surprise you as you pull slow and steady on the trigger, just keep your focus on the target. As you do you will learn one of the most important things we can learn as a man, the importance of keeping a laser focus. Brothers, there are so many things out there working to take your focus off of the mission given to you by the Lord. There will always be hot women trying to distract you, there will always be addictions waiting to destroy your life, there will be constant acts of satan and his army to knock you off course. But losing our focus cannot be an option. No matter what, keep your eyes on the target of finishing strong and faithful everyday by living in SOULCON."

As we all walk to the line to pick up our rifles and shoot, Bugsly stops us. "Before you grab your rifles, I forgot to tell you the physical fitness challenge of this to help you mentally overcome external pressures. Before you shoot give me 30 burpees, 30 jumping jacks, 30 push-ups and then grab your rifles, and you have two minutes to fire 25 rounds. We will do this five times this morning and the top five men will be able to keep one of these brand new AR-15s. Just remember, focus your mind, calm your heart-rate, and don't allow any negative thoughts to creep in. Let's do it! Kick butt team!"

> *"I'm not saying that I have this all together, that I have it made. But I am well on my way, reaching out for Christ, who has so wondrously reached out for me. Friends, don't get me wrong: By no means do I count myself an expert in all of this, but I've got my eye on the goal, where God is beckoning us onward— to Jesus. I'm off and running, and I'm not turning back. So let's keep focused on that goal, those of us who want everything God has for us. If any of you have something else in mind, something less than total commitment, God will clear your blurred vision—you'll see it yet! Now that we're on the right track, let's stay on it.*
> Philippians 3:12-16 (The Message)

DAILY CHALLENGE

Do 30 burpees, 30 jumping jacks, 30 push-ups and then hold the plank for 30 seconds. Focus on controlling your mind and emotions during the plank. Visualize shooting a rifle on the range like in the devotional. Use your imagination to put you on the shooting range and take the pain away from the plank.

DAY 41
ALL IN

If anyone desires to come after Me, let him deny himself, and take up his cross daily, and follow Me.

Luke 9:23 (NKJV)

Walking into the room where we will have our graduation tomorrow, my heart is flooded with joy as I think about seeing my family. I can't wait to share with them everything I've learned, and most importantly I can't wait for them to see the man I've become in Christ. For our team, today is an easy day, the focus of today is to make sure everything is packed up and ready to go. Tonight will be our last night in the SOULCON Training Center. So many different emotions come over me as I think about the friendships I've made, and the lessons I've learned. I continue thinking and walking over for the pep talk from the Founder of SOULCON.

I take a seat with the guys, as the Founder and Commander Bugsly walk in.

"It's great to see you guys" the Founder says, "I hope you've had an incredible journey during this challenging time at SOULCON. Learning about your soul is not an easy journey, so I want you to know I'm proud of you! Learning the power of carrying your cross and the dangers of letting the flesh eat from the fork that feeds it is crucial as soldiers of Jesus. I hope during your stay the Lord revealed to you the joy in following Him and the dangers of walking in the flesh.

For our last topic before graduation I want to share with you something I want you to carry out in every area of life. I want you to remember being an elite soldier of Jesus is an everyday, all of the time thing. There is no compartmentalizing your walk in the Spirit. From housework, to helping with laundry, to praying for the sick and sharing the Good News, we need Jesus in every area. He desires to help us serve at our highest capacity, and He knows we will get hungry, tired, and exhausted. He is just looking for men like you who will identify the weakness of your flesh and focus your mind, will and emotions on walking in the power of the Spirit. Men, being tired is okay, going hungry is okay, and being exhausted is okay, life is a constant challenge and it will never be easy so don't expect it to be. If you find yourself taking the 'easy way out' repent and lean back into the discipline. Embrace the pain of leaving it all on the field for Jesus. Train your body and soul to be ready for those hard times that WILL come by growing in the Spirit each day. Sow seeds to optimal health daily so when you get placed on a certain mission you're fit and ready to accomplish what God places in front of you. Again, I am proud of you all. Before graduation tomorrow please take time to read through Mark 6:30-56 and look at a time when Jesus sees the mission as more important than the comfort of His disciples. Ask the Holy Spirit to work in your heart a joy for living as a sacrifice of service like this in every area of life.

See you guys in the morning!"

"The apostles returned to Jesus from their ministry tour and told him all they had done and taught. Then Jesus said, 'Let's go off by ourselves to a quiet place and rest awhile.' He said this because there were so many people coming and going that Jesus and his apostles didn't even have time to eat.

So they left by boat for a quiet place, where they could be alone. But many people recognized them and saw them leaving, and people from many towns ran ahead along the shore and got there ahead of them. Jesus saw the huge crowd as he stepped from the boat, and he had compassion on them because they were like sheep without a shepherd. So he began teaching them many things.

Late in the afternoon his disciples came to him and said, 'This is a remote place, and it's already getting late. Send the crowds away so they can go to the nearby farms and villages and buy something to eat.'

But Jesus said, 'You feed them.'

'With what?' they asked. 'We'd have to work for months to earn enough money to buy food for all these people!'

'How much bread do you have?' he asked. 'Go and find out.'

They came back and reported, 'We have five loaves of bread and two fish.'

Then Jesus told the disciples to have the people sit down in groups on the green grass.

So they sat down in groups of fifty or a hundred. Jesus took the five loaves and two fish, looked up toward heaven, and blessed them. Then, breaking the loaves into pieces, he kept giving the bread to the disciples so they could distribute it to the people. He also divided the fish for everyone to share. They all ate as much as they wanted, and afterward, the disciples picked up twelve baskets of leftover bread and fish. A total of 5,000 men and their families were fed.

Immediately after this, Jesus insisted that his disciples get back into the boat and head across the lake to Bethsaida, while he sent the people home. After telling everyone good-bye, he went up into the hills by himself to pray.

Late that night, the disciples were in their boat in the middle of the lake, and Jesus was alone on land. He saw that they were in serious trouble, rowing hard and struggling against the wind and waves. About three o'clock in the morning Jesus came toward them, walking on the water. He intended to go past them, but when they saw him walking on the water, they cried out in terror, thinking he was a ghost. They were all terrified when they saw him.

But Jesus spoke to them at once. 'Don't be afraid,' he said. 'Take courage! I am here!' Then he climbed into the boat, and the wind stopped. They were totally amazed, for they still didn't understand the significance of the miracle of the loaves. Their hearts were too hard to take it in.

After they had crossed the lake, they landed at Gennesaret. They brought the boat to shore and climbed out. The people recognized Jesus at once, and they ran throughout the whole area, carrying sick people on mats to wherever they heard he was. Wherever he went—in villages, cities, or the countryside—they brought the sick out to the marketplaces. They begged him to let the sick touch at least the fringe of his robe, and all who touched him were healed."
Mark 6:30-56 (NLT)

DAILY CHALLENGE

Ask the Spirit to teach you from this text about the importance of following His leading more than the desires of your flesh. Ask the Lord to continue to prepare you for service like the example of these disciples in this text.

Greater love has no one than this, than to lay down one's life for his friends.

John 15:13 (NKJV)

Well, today is the day. I roll out of bed and hit my knees with a big smile. I pray the Lord's Prayer, and I spend a little extra time thanking God for this journey. I sit and think about everything I've learned and I ask the Holy Spirit to help me disciple other men with these principals and practices when I get home. I lift up my family in prayer and ask for God's peace to be over every part of our day. I can hardly wait to see my family…

As I finish praying, I sit up and grab a cup of coffee, and I open my daily devotional and read the SOULCON Creed:

"We live in such a way that no one will stumble because of us, and no one will find fault with our ministry. In everything we do, we show that we are true ministers of God. We patiently endure troubles and hardships and calamities of every kind. We have been beaten, been put in prison, faced angry mobs, worked to exhaustion, endured sleepless nights, and gone without food. We prove ourselves by our purity, our understanding, our patience, our kindness, by the Holy Spirit within us, and by our sincere love. We faithfully preach the truth. God's power is working in us. We use the weapons of righteousness in the right hand for attack and the left hand for defense. We serve God whether people honor us or despise us, whether they slander us or praise us." 2 Corinthians 6:3-8a (NLT)

As I read through this I commit to fully live this out in my life. This challenge is not something that finishes today, but it begins a new lifestyle for me as an elite disciple of Jesus Christ. A disciple not afraid of discomfort, not afraid of long days and nights, not afraid to go all in and be a living sacrifice for Jesus.

I look over at the clock and see that in less than an hour I will be able to see my family for the first time in six weeks. I can hardly contain the excitement, but there are a few things I have to get done first. I hurry through getting ready and make sure everything is packed and ready to go, including my sweet new AR-15 with the brand new case from placing in the top five in the shooting challenge.

As I walk out of my room for the last time, a wave of emotions hit me. "Please Lord, let this be a lasting transformation in me. Please help me to not forget this lifestyle. Help me be the man of valor that you have called me to be, the one I saw that I can be during my stay here." I finish my prayer and shut the door for the last time. Tyler and Alfred call my name to join them for the last walk to the grinder. I proudly grab my bags and jog over to join them for the walk.

"Good morning brothers, you ready?!

"I'm ready!" Tyler says. "This has been one incredible ride, huh?"

"Oh man," Alfred says, "I cannot believe everything we went through. I mean a team ice bath, skydiving, shooting rifles and even confessing deep sins with each other. Thank you guys for going through this with me. I love you both and I look forward to taking this lifestyle back to our family and friends."

"Amen," I say back to Alfred.

Just then we see Commander Bugsly and the Founder at the grinder. They are smiling ear-to-ear. We are too.

"Good morning brothers!" Bugsly shouts to our team. "I have to be honest, I'm going to miss you guys! This is one of the best and worst days of our training. I always get so excited to see teams finish, but I hate to see them leave. The encouragement the Lord always gives me is that you're all world changers, you have refined your focus, and now, in my opinion, you're more prepared than ever to carry out your specific missions from Jesus on earth. In that I rest. I look forward to the day we get to feast together in Heaven. The day we get to look back at everything we did in the Spirit to serve God and His creation on this earth. We will be proud veterans at that point, and I cannot wait to hear your war stories. Until then, continue to serve everyone with the healthiest body possible. Let nothing control your soul except the Spirit. Live as SOULCON warriors until the end. Finish strong!"

"Amen!" the Founder says. "Like Commander said, we will miss you and we're all proud of you here. We consider everyone who finishes this challenge an elite warrior for Jesus and I am honored to serve Jesus with you. Thank you for committing this time to learn the SOULCON lifestyle! Before we run over to graduation and see our families, let me read one of my favorite quotes to you from Charles Spurgeon. I hope this rings in your ears until we all meet again with the Lord…

'If by excessive labor, we die before the average age of man, worn out in the Master's service, then glory be to God, we shall have so much less of earth and so much more of Heaven . . . It is our duty and our privilege to exhaust our lives for Jesus. We are not to be living specimens of men in fine preservation, but living sacrifices, whose lot is to be consumed.'"

FINAL CHALLENGE

Encourage one other man, or a group of men to take on this challenge. Be intentional. Never forget some of the lessons you learned from the Lord during this time. One of the best things we can do as men is to encourage other men to live sold out for Jesus, as true followers of Christ. Continue to soldier on and finish every day knowing you left it all on the field for Jesus.

Congratulations Soulcon Graduate!
You're ready for the next challenge, Soulcon Warrior Elite.
Make sure to grab your copy at soulcon.com.

WEEK 06 RESULTS

Congratulations Soulcon Graduate!
You're ready for the next challenge, Soulcon Warrior Elite.
Make sure to grab your copy at soulcon.com.

Be sure to share your results and encourage others
going through the challenge on the SOULCON App.

WEEK 06 REFLECTIONS

Congratulations Soulcon Graduate!
You're ready for the next challenge, Soulcon Warrior Elite.
Make sure to grab your copy at soulcon.com.

Be sure to share your reflections and encourage others
going through the challenge on the SOULCON App.

SOULCON OPTIONAL MEAL PLANS

These meal plans are strictly options that I have provided. If you have specific nutritional needs or physical limitations, please consult with your physician before you start this challenge. Again, these are just options that I have provided for you as guidelines throughout this challenge.

For all of your meals make sure you space them out 2.5-3hrs apart for maximal results.

Option 1 (except for Hell Week)

Monday (Military Time)

Meal 1 0730	1 Packet Lower Sugar Oatmeal(1/2 cup dry of Oats) 6 eggs (6 whites)
Meal 2 1030	1 scoop of protein with an apple
Meal 3 1330	Tuna Pack with 1 bag of veggie steamers and 1 cup (cooked) of brown rice
Meal 4 1600	1 scoop of protein and an apple
Meal 5 1830	6oz Top Sirloin and veggies
Meal 6 2100	10 Almonds

Tuesday

Meal 1 0730	1 Packet Lower Sugar Oatmeal (1/2 cup dry of Oats) 6 egg whites
Meal 2 1030	1 scoop of protein w/an apple
Meal 3 1330	1 packets of lower sugar oatmeal with 6 egg whites
Meal 4 1600	1 tablespoon of natural PB and 1 scoop of protein and an apple
Meal 5 1830	Chicken Breast with a salad with light balsamic vinaigrette
Meal 6 2100	1 scoops of protein with 10 almonds

Wednesday

Meal 1	0730	2 Pieces of Whole Wheat Toast with 6 egg whites
Meal 2	1030	1 scoop of protein with an apple
Meal 3	1330	6 egg whites and 1 packet of lower sugar oatmeal
Meal 4	1600	1 tablespoon of natural PB and 1 scoop of protein and an apple
Meal 5	1830	6 oz Lean Ground Turkey Meat and veggies
Meal 6	2100	10 almonds

Thursday

Meal 1	0730	2 Packets Lower Sugar Oatmeal(1/2 cup dry of Oats) 9 eggs (3 yolks and 6 whites)
Meal 2	1030	1 scoop of protein with an apple
Meal 3	1330	Tuna Pack with 1 bag of veggie steamers and 1 cup (cooked) of brown rice
Meal 4	1600	Pure Protein bar and an apple
Meal 5	1830	Tilapia with veggies
Meal 6	2100	10 almonds

Friday

Meal 1	0730	1 Packets Lower Sugar Oatmeal(1/2 cup dry of Oats) 6 eggs (3 yolks and 3 whites)
Meal 2	1030	1 scoop of protein with an apple
Meal 3	1330	Chicken Breast Sandwich with whole wheat bread
Meal 4	1600	Protein bar and an apple
Meal 5	1830	Top Sirloin and veggies (any kind is good)
Meal 6	2100	10 almonds

Saturday
Feast Day

Sunday

Meal 1	0730	1 Packet Lower Sugar Oatmeal(1/2 cup dry of Oats) and 6 egg whites
Meal 2	1030	1 scoop of protein with an apple
Meal 3	1330	6 oz Lean Ground Turkey Meat with ½ cup of brown rice, and veggies
Meal 4	1600	1 tablespoon of natural PB and 1 scoop of protein

and an apple
Meal 5 1830   Tilapia with veggies
Meal 6 2100   10 almonds

Option 2 (except for Hell Week)

Monday   (Military Time)

Meal 1 0700   1 Packet Lower Sugar Oatmeal 3 eggs whites
Meal 2 1000   Apple and a protein shake
Meal 3 1300   Chicken Breast w/1 bag of broccoli steamers and ½ brown rice
Meal 4 1530   15 healthy unsalted nuts with an apple
Meal 5 1900   4-6oz lean meat and veggies (any kind is good) Just no carbs
Meal 6 2100   10 unsalted nuts (optional)

Tuesday
Meal 1 0700   3 eggs (1 yolk and 2 whites) made with low fat mozzarella for an omelet w/ 1/2 Grapefruit and 1 waffle
Meal 2 1000   Apple and a protein shake
Meal 3 1300   Tuna packet of any flavor with veggies and an orange
Meal 4 1530   15 healthy unsalted nuts with an apple
Meal 5 1900   Chicken Breast with a salad with light balsamic vinaigrette.
Meal 6 2100   10 unsalted nuts (optional)

Wednesday

Meal 1 0700   1 Packet Lower Sugar Oatmeal 3 eggs whites
Meal 2 1000   Grapefruit
Meal 3 1300   Chicken Breast with a sweet potato 1 bag of broccoli steamers
Meal 4 1500   Protein shake and 10 unsalted nuts
Meal 5 1930   4-6oz lean meat and veggies (any kind is good) Just no carbs
Meal 6 2100   10 unsalted nuts (optional)

Thursday
Meal 1 0700   4 egg whites with 1 packet of sugar free oatmeal
Meal 2 1000   Apple and a protein shake
Meal 3 1300   Tuna packet of any flavor with veggies and a ½ cup
              of brown rice
Meal 4 1530   15 healthy unsalted nuts with an apple
Meal 5 1900   Lean meat with a salad with light balsamic
              vinaigrette
Meal 6 2100   10 unsalted nuts (optional)

Friday
Meal 1 0700   1 Packet Lower Sugar Oatmeal 3 eggs whites
Meal 2 1000   Apple
Meal 3 1300   Chicken Breast w/1 bag of broccoli steamers and a
              sweet potato
Meal 4 1530   Protein shake with an apple and 10 cashews
Meal 5 1900   4-6oz lean meat and veggies (any kind is good) Just
              no carbs

Saturday
Feast Day

Sunday

Meal 1 0730   4 Egg Whites with veggies (omelet) w/ 1 packet
              lower sugar oatmeal
Meal 2 1000   Apple
Meal 3 1230   Chicken Breast with a sweet potato ½ bag of
              broccoli steamers
Meal 4 1430   1 Orange and a protein shake
Meal 5 1700   Lean meat and veggies
Meal 6 2000   15 nuts

ABOUT CODY BOBAY

Cody Bobay met Jesus as his Lord and Savior at 18 years old while on Active Duty in the US Navy as a Naval Aircrewman. From that point of salvation to this point in ministry, Cody lives to tell about the Good News of Jesus Christ. Cody and his wife of eleven years, and two kids count it a honor to destroy the work of the Enemy in Jesus Name, daily.

Cody is the author of Soulcon Challenge, Soulcon Warrior Elite and the founder of Soulcon Ministries. He passionately pleas with every Christian man to link together as special forces soldiers for Jesus Christ and advance the Kingdom by force.

Jesus is coming soon.
We have to make the most of every day.

Congratulations Soulcon Graduate!
You're ready for the next challenge, Soulcon Warrior Elite.
Make sure to grab your copy at soulcon.com.